LEARNING AND VISUAL COMMUNICATION

Learning and Visual Communication

DAVID SLESS

A HALSTED PRESS BOOK

CROOM HELM LONDON
JOHN WILEY & SONS
New York — Toronto

© 1981 David Sless
Croom Helm Ltd, 2-10 St John's Road, London SW11

Published in the U.S.A. and Canada
by Halsted Press, a Division of
John Wiley & Sons, Inc., New York
LC Number:

British Library Cataloguing in Publication Data

Sless, David
    Learning and visual communication. - (New patterns
    of learning series)
    1. Visual Perception
    2. Perceptual learning
    I. Title II. Series
    152.1'4 BF241

    ISBN 0-7099-2319-8

Library of Congress Cataloging in Publication Data

Sless, David.
    Learning and visual communication.

    (New patterns of learning)
    "A Halsted Press book."
    Bibliography: p. 189
    Includes index.
    1. Learning, Psychology of. 2. Visual perception.
3. Interpersonal communication. I. Title. II. Series.
BF318.S54 1981   370.15'5   81-6417
ISBN 0-470-27231-7 (Halsted Press)   AACR2

Printed in Great Britain by
Biddles Ltd, Guildford, Surrey

CONTENTS

To Toni, Justine, Hannah, Eva and Georgia

NEW PATTERNS OF LEARNING

The Purpose of this Series

This series of books is intended to provide readable introductions to trends and areas of current thinking in education. Each book will be of interest to all educators, trainers and administrators reponsible for the implementation of educational policies and programmes in higher, further and continuing education.

The books are designed for easy access of information and contain bibliographies of key works to enable the reader to pursue selected areas in more depth should he or she so wish.

This book offers guidance to all those concerned with visual forms of communication by drawing on relevant research in psychology, philosophy, semiotics, cultural analysis, education and media studies. It is written by David Sless who is Senior Lecturer in Visual and Verbal Communication at the Flinders University of South Australia.

P.J. Hills
Leicester

PREFACE

This book is an attempt to provide a way of thinking about visual communication, and it is written specifically for those with an interest, but no specialist knowledge, in the subject. The emphasis is on the educational uses of visual communication though the ideas have a much wider application to our understanding of communication in general. I have followed certain principles in writing this book, which are intended to help the reader. Wherever possible I have avoided specialist terminology; where this has been unavoidable I have given detailed definitions which are summarised in the glossary. This is not a comprehensive book but a development of main ideas; evidence is only introduced by way of example and the reader in search of greater detail will find many useful sources in the bibliography. In citing references I have given only those which are either directly quoted or substantially relevant to the argument. I have avoided the common practice of trying to legitimise statements by indicating that someone (preferably famous) has said it before. If I were to adopt that practice in this area then every sentence could have a string of names to it, and the reader would be burdened with a much longer set of references. The references given will, directly or indirectly, lead the reader to the major areas of relevance. Finally, I have presented ideas in as economical a manner as possible in the belief that the imaginative reader will be able to elaborate the ideas more fully without losing the main thread. Above all I hope this brief book will stimulate fresh thought and action in visual communication.

David Sless
Adelaide

ACKNOWLEDGEMENTS

Being the author is a dubious privilege: it ensures that someone can be held responsible for the faults of the work. In so far as this work is worthy of the readers' attention, the credit must go to all those who have shaped the author's thought, provided the environment in which the work developed, and helped in the intricate task of bringing the work to fruition. If this book is lucid, clear and readable the credit should go to Ruth Shrensky who carefully, meticulously and with great intelligence transformed my clumsy prose as well as allowing my obsessive preoccupation with this book to dominate our family life over the past eighteen months.

My deepest intellectual gratitude goes to Professor Patrick Meredith who first inspired my interest in communication. Many colleagues have played a part in shaping my ideas. Flora Pearson, Richard Rainer and Peter Welton helped me greatly to formulate my early ideas about visual communication and I hope this book reflects something of the spirit of our intense collaboration. My thanks to all the students, over the years, who have taught me so much.

I would like to thank Paul Duncum, Vincent Megaw, Ted Nunan and Val Presley for their helpful comments on various chapters of this book. I have enjoyed the privilege of being supported throughout the writing of this book by the Flinders University of South Australia. I would particularly like to thank the Study Leave Committee for allowing me time in which I was able to initiate this project. My thanks to Frances Kelly, my agent, for her efforts and encouragement and to Philip Hills for his patience and support during the writing of this book. My thanks also to Lis Jansson who exercised much care and attention when typing the manuscript.

Finally, I would like to thank Flinders University Photographic Service who prepared many of the illustrations for publication and Amanda Biggs for her meticulous work on the bibliography and the index.

1 THE THINKING EYE

Introduction

This book is about the role of visual communication in learning. A wide range of materials which convey information visually are used as part of the education process, and at no other time has it been possible to take advantage of such a rich variety of visual experience and knowledge with so much ease; cheap printing, photography and electronic processes are widely available. But this is not a book about the hardware of visual communication, nor is it about the management of that hardware, although indirectly it has something to say about these. It is wholly concerned with how we think about visual communication. How we use visual material in education depends to a large extent on how we conceptualise it; what we expect it to do depends on what we assume it to be capable of.

There is no single source, no authority, no body of knowledge sufficiently well organised into a discipline which could be described as the subject of visual communication. If one is foolhardy enough to develop an interest in a subject which crosses many of the usual subject boundaries then one must also face the consequence of such an enterprise — namely one has to develop a framework, an intellectual focus that enables one to make sense of all the disparate fields which contribute to our understanding of that area of interest. This then is an attempt to provide such a framework. In doing so I will challenge many of the presuppositions that underlie current practice and teaching, but my intent is constructive. Visual communication is one of the most exciting and potentially useful tools in education if we can understand how to exploit its richness.

Theory and Knowledge about Vision

I will begin this exploration of visual communication with a close look at our knowledge and assumptions about vision. As vision is the central process around which is constructed the overall process of visual communication, it is useful to begin an account of the subject from this focal point.

15

The history of ideas about vision is one of the most fascinating chapters in the development of human thought, within which we can identify two contrasting approaches. Ideas stemming from the classical philosophical tradition separate vision from thinking and treat each as discrete processes. This separation has been the basis of most physiological and psychological research into vision and it is also at the heart of the popular notion of vision. Vision is the province of the eyes, a purely sensory process; thought is entirely a mental activity; and the two are logically and biologically distinct.

In contrast, the tradition of thought stemming from the work of Kant (1781) acknowledges no such distinction. Vision and thinking are one process; they cannot be separated, either logically or physiologically. It will be clear from the title of this chapter, 'The Thinking Eye', that I take this latter view.

What is wrong then with the traditional approach?

First, the eye is not biologically separate from the brain. It is actually part of the same organ; or more accurately, the brain is part of the eye. In the development of the embryo (and in all probability the evolution of the species), 'the eyes are first to appear, the brain being a subsequent outgrowth' (Polyak, 1968, p. 767). In structural terms the eyes have not grown out of the brain, the brain has receded from the eyes.

Vision is the instigator of thought, not its handmaiden. Neural tissue developed in order to make use of incoming visual information. The evolutionary catalyst for the development of the brain was the need to process visual information. Vision is the seat of intellect.

Secondly, the eye is not a recorder of visual information, even though mechanical optical devices have often been used as an analogy. Early studies of the eye progressed as a consequence of the development of optics, when Kepler realised that the eye contained a lens whose function is to focus the incoming light on to the retina at the back of the eye. When later investigators peeled back the opaque coat protecting the retina, they saw a small inverted image of whatever the eyeball was pointing at. This retinal image was to have a profound but misleading effect on the course of research and thinking, for the optical similarities between the eye and the camera provide only a very superficial basis for understanding vision, one fraught with difficulties. It is necessary to explain what role this retinal image plays, enabling us to see. The classical tradition, in separating vision from thinking, generated the idea of a 'mind's eye' which looked at the retinal image. The problem was that you were left with the need to explain the way the mind's eye worked and so on in an endless regress.

Another problem with the analogy is that the eye has a very poor lens and the cone of clear vision is only 2°wide. (You can test this by holding a coin out in front of you, fixating the centre and at the same time trying to read the date at the edge. It cannot be done unless the angle between the eye, centre and edge of the coin is less than two degrees.)

Yet another complication arises as a consequence of the characteristic movement of the eye. The eye is never at rest. It moves in a series of jumps and between jumps it has a constant tremor, so that the focused light is continually moving over the retinal field. A photographic plate under such conditions would simply be a blur. If the image is stabilised under experimental conditions the retinal cells become satiated and the object on which the eye is focused appears to merge or disappear into the background (Pritchard, 1961).

This blurred retinal image has two other technical defects. At the point where the optic nerve leaves the eye there are no light-sensitive cells so that effectively there is a hole in the retinal image; and the image is inverted. Yet none of these facts is registered in our perception which is of a panoramic, stable, unperforated, upright world. So the retinal image explains nothing but in its turn generates a whole series of difficulties that require explanation.

If this were not enough, the retina itself, far from being a simple array of light-sensitive receptors, is an intricate network of cells which organise the incoming visual information before transmitting it along the optic nerve fibre. There are over 100 million light-sensitive cells in the retina. There is also a series of cells, called bipolar cells, which interconnect across groups of light-sensitive cells, and connect these to the ganglion cells that make up the optic nerve fibre. There are only 800,000 ganglion cells which of itself suggests that some condensation or recoding of the retinal information takes place. In fact with the development of microelectrode techniques it has been possible to compare the information being presented to the eye with the neurological activity in the brain, and it has been discovered that singe neurons are 'feature specific'; that is, each one responds to a particular line or a particular direction of movement rather than to a particular focus on the retina. The analogy between eye and camera must finally be laid to rest. The eye's constructive integrative ability must cast serious doubt on the idea that vision is a sensory process pure and simple.

However the attempt to maintain the innocence of vision finds other than empirical grounds to sustain itself.

The sense-datum theory suggests that the raw stuff of vision are patches of light and dark, colours and shapes, which through some unspecified process of inference are transformed into our perceptions. The problem with this is that to talk about patches of light, dark and colour is even then to invoke a series of abstractions. There are many ways of dividing the light around us into units and each different method involves different abstracting principles. There can be no such thing as 'pure' vision. The question then arises as to which abstracting principles must be logically prior to all others and this is a philosophical problem rather than a factual one.

It was towards this problem that Kant addressed his attention, by suggesting that there could be no experience at all unless the mind ordered its information, and the mind could not order experience without some prior framework in which to do the ordering. Although Kant did not actually concern himself with the problem of perception, mainly wrestling with the nature of thinking, his arguments can be used with equal force to resolve the paradoxes of vision outlined above.

Despite our impression of completeness the mechanisms of vision are structured to operate selectively. The narrow cone of clear vision subtended from the eye means that only selected aspects of the visual field can be examined at any one time.

The Optic Array

It would be a great mistake to think of the eyes as peculiarly inefficient organs for performing the task of making sense of the visible world. The human eye is the end-product of a long evolutionary process in which the organism has adapted to the environment. The eyes more than any other single sensory system have enabled organisms to orientate themselves with respect to their physical environment. This ecological view of vision has revealed an important basis of the way we structure visual experience. Light arriving at the eye from the objects in the world does so in a coherent form. It travels in straight lines and as we or the objects move with respect to each other the light changes in a consistent manner. As we walk past a series of posts numbered 1 to 5, the light coming from the posts always presents a consistent form. At no point does the order of the posts alter. It will always be 1, 2, 3, 4, 5 or 5, 4, 3, 2, 1, never say, 3, 1, 4, 2, 5. Moreover we can predict what the information available to the eye will be from any point of regard because light behaves consistently. This coherence, or set of rules, is there as the basis for any organism's orientation in space. It is called the optic array.

So far we do not need Kant's revolutionary notions of the way the mind structures experience. An ordered structure exists in the environment. That however is only part of the explanation since the organism must either learn the rules which govern the transformations of the optic array as either the organism or objects in the world move, or else those rules must be built into the visual system. Either way, there does have to be a mental ability to 'read' the optic array. At the very minimum it is necessary to postulate some readiness on the part of an organism to learn about the optic array. However even if it is assumed that some satisfactory account can be given of this and that the overall framework of perception is guaranteed by the coherent structure of light, it still remains necessary to explain how it is that an organism selects certain features of the environment for attention rather than others. All the optic array tells us is that whatever we look at will behave consistently with respect to our own movement through space, and that if it moves we will be able to read its movement in a consistent way. What it does not tell us is which detectable feature within the enormous range of detectable features within any optic array we should attend to. For that we need some other explanation.

Schemata and Objectification

It is here that we turn to Kant's notion of *Schema* and its contemporary elaboration. Simply put, schematism is the process of organising experience. It is a concept with very wide application since it not only allows for the organising of visual experience but of all mental activity. In this text we will only be concerned with a limited range of schemata, those relating to visual communication, but these are themselves embedded within the general schemata that determine the way we select and use all visual information. These in their turn are embedded within the general schemata that determine the pattern of behaviour of the whole organism.

Here we have a key notion in understanding vision as a thinking process. The eye's selective organising capacity is directed by schemata and these schemata are learnt. An example of the operation at one level of schemata can be seen in Figure 1. It may not be readily

Figure 1: Hidden Figure

apparent what the figure represents, that is you may not have the necessary schema to hand that will enable you to read it. If I provide you with the necessary schema by telling you that is a picture of a cow you may now be able to read the picture. If its form still eludes you look at Figure 2 and you will find an outline that will give you the correct schema. It should now be possible to make sense of the picture. The transformation that has occurred is a dramatic demonstration of the mutability of vision and it bears close analysis.

First, the schema is a framework which enables us to select which fragments are to be pieced together and which are to be ignored. Secondly, once the schema is established it is remarkably stable, so much so that it is difficult if not impossible to look at the picture in the way we did before the schema was formed. Thirdly and most interestingly the change that occurred seemed to do so before one's eyes.

I say 'before one's eyes' because that is the impression we had. We know that the picture has not changed and yet there is a strong impression that a change has taken place outside ourselves. The only change is in our visual thinking, but we tend to externalise that change. We objectify it. We treat it as if it were part of an objective world outside ourselves which we are observing. This notion of objectification is extremely important in our understanding of visual thinking and the peculiar learning problems posed by visual communications. I shall have occasion to return to this central issue in later sections.

The main lesson of this example is that vision is a mutable process. The extent of its mutability is an open question because the history of vision has been dominated by the erroneous view that vision is a sensory process, hence unchangeable, merely recording 'what is there'.

Visual Literacy

In many areas of knowledge where observation forms a central role, one of the primary tasks of the educator is to develop in the student an ability to structure, organise and give meaning to visible evidence. Many forms of visual narrative demonstration and explanation exist as common cultural objects in print, photography, film and electronic media. The expertise which has led to these has not come from the psychologist's laboratory but from the accumulated traditions of practice in the arts of communication. Our ability to read this material is almost taken for granted, but it does have to be learnt and the sophistication with which we can accomplish that task is proportional to the amount of effort we expend in educating vision. Visual literacy and fluency are skills, discernible and distinguishable from literacy and numeracy which form the backbone of our educational system, but they are not subjected to anything like the intensity of teaching that students are given in language and mathematics.

The skill of reading the written language is an example of a highly specialised visual skill. But we only have a scant knowledge of how it is mastered and the processes that make it possible. 'Rapid reading represents an achievement as impossible in theory as it is commonplace in practice' (Neisser, 1967, p. 137). If we could imagine a non-literate society armed with our current knowledge of psychology reacting to the proposal that reading were possible, we would expect them to dismiss the idea as a wild fancy. This bizarre and unlikely fable is an important caution. First, we should not put too much faith in current psychological theory which cannot even explain very common-place visual skills; and secondly we should not assume that the present level of visual ability is at its highest point of development. Laboratory studies can only measure existing skilled performance. It is not possible on the basis of present knowledge to predict what sophisticated visual abilities could be developed.

So the implications of vision as a mutable process are far reaching and the psychological and philosophical theories which lead us to this conclusion must in a certain sense now be abandoned, because they can only take us part of the way towards an understanding of the educational role of vision and visual material. They will remain in the background of our considerations. The central concepts of schema and objectification will be used throughout this text, but we will refer increasingly to those areas where visual expertise is of a practical kind and the knowledge employed is very often the tacit knowledge of the practitioner.

Figure 2: Hidden Figure Revealed

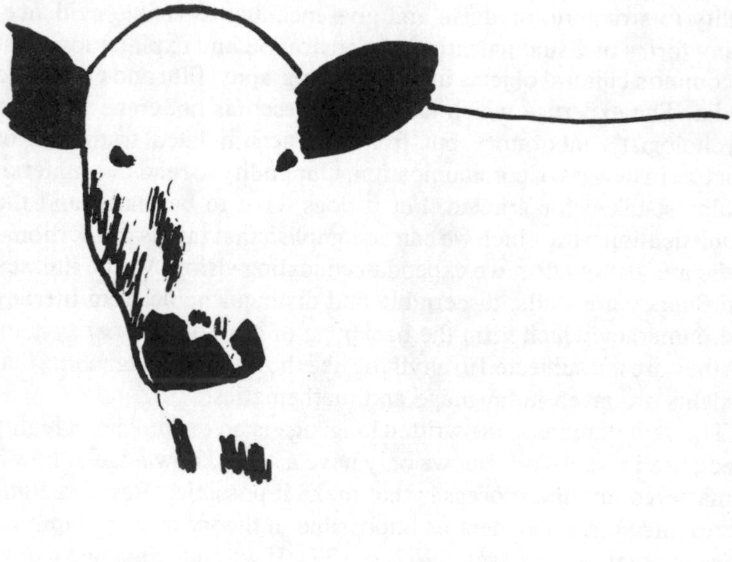

2 COMMUNICATION

Introduction

In this chapter I shall guide the reader towards a framework for discussing the elusive process of visual communication — for if vision may have seemed mutable as a consequence of our discussion in Chapter 1 then visual communication will seem capricious. Visual communication is a major transmitter of our cultural heritage, second only to the spoken word. The printed word, paintings, drawings, sculpture, photography, cartography, charts, diagrams, graphs, film and television are all visual forms of communication and they depend centrally on the complex process of visual cognition. It is in many ways a paradox that a process which so powerfully influences the continuity of knowledge, and the traditions of practice and belief from one generation to the next, should be so unpredictable.

There has been a long tradition of enquiry into visual communication. Some people, such as art historians or cartographers, have an obvious interest in discussing visual communication seriously. Others such as philosophers and mathematicians might seem less likely inquirers into this realm, but such is the utility, ubiquity, ambiguity and presumed power of visual communication that there is hardly a discipline which has not participated in the research. This in itself generates the problem of different viewpoints and terminologies which make any generalised synthesis inordinately difficult. In relating visual communication to learning, one faces the special task of bringing something with wide cultural use and traditions of practice into contact with the specialist fields of pedagogic theory and practice.

In embarking on this course I have adopted a pragmatic approach. The framework I am going to elaborate in these pages must stand or fall by its usefulness in teaching. If it aids the management of the learning environment and helps the learner within it, if it lays the foundation for identifying learning problems and provides a basis for resolving them, then it will have succeeded. I will not, in what follows, trace the development of this framework from its origins in communication theory, nor will I argue the theoretical merits of the framework against other possibilities — the interested reader can trace the various strands of argument from sources given in the bibliography. I shall only mention directly those sources which have been especially

23

formative or those which I regard as especially misleading.

Because my intent is practical, I will be at pains to maintain a very strict control on the use of specialist vocabulary. My attitude towards educational theory will at times be somewhat irreverent — this is because I believe that much of what passes for educational theory is of dubious value when it comes to the day-to-day management of learning and teaching.

In this chapter I will give a very general account of the process of communication. Only when that is complete will we be ready to look at visual communication as an aspect of education.

The Two Faces of Communication

Most discussions on communication begin by stating that there are certain basic units involved in the process. These typically are the sender, the message and the receiver (see Figure 3). Sometimes this

Figure 3: The Basic Units of Communication

Figure 4: Elaboration of the Basic Units of Communication

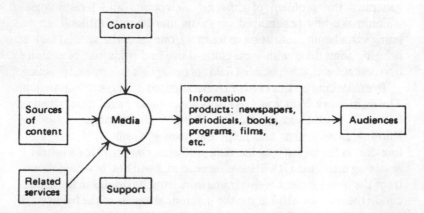

Source: Wilbur Schram, *Men, Messages and Media* (Harper & Row, New York, 1973), p. 144.

basic model is elaborated for special purposes (see Figure 4), but even though the terminology may differ and the emphasis or degree of elaboration may vary, the fundamental pattern remains the same with three discernible aspects concerned respectively with the production of a message, the message itself, and its reception. This classic model goes back to the first treatise on the subject, Aristotle's *Rhetorica*.

Despite the pedigree and age of this model, it will not be used in this text. Instead I shall adopt a completely different strategy and discuss communication in terms of *two relations*: the author/message relation and the audience/message relation, as in Figure 5 (I use the terms 'author' and 'audience' as generic terms to cover any kind of message producer and message receiver respectively). As a formal procedure this means that from now on I will always declare whether I am going to consider a particular message in its audience context or in its author context — the message will not be treated as a distinct entity which can be analysed separately from author or audience.

Figure 5: New Model of the Communication Process

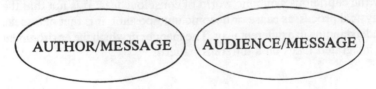

The Discovery of Pulsars

It is very difficult to extract ourselves from a continuous process of communication and find out what is happening. If we wish to exchange our thoughts on the nature of communication we must use the very process we are seeking to understand as the means for doing so. We are therefore fortunate in that we can strip away the complexities which surround normal communication, by examining an abnormal case — a phenomenon that was for a short time thought to be a message (but turned out not to be).

In 1968 a group of radio astronomers discovered, almost by accident, the existence of a radio source which showed regular fluctuations in energy. Nothing like it had ever been discovered before and there was a flurry of excitement and speculation about its origins and causes.

As the days went by the excitement rose when we found that the pulses were coming from a body no larger than a planet situated relatively close to us among the nearer stars of our galaxy. Were the pulses some kind of message from another civilization? This possibility was entertained only for lack of an obvious natural explanation for signals that seemed so artificial. (Hewish, 1968)

Here is the knife edge of the distinction between what is and what is not communication; on one side a natural phenomenon without acceptable explanation and on the other a message with an unknown sender and unknown meaning. For the brief period that the scientists entertained the latter possibility their line of enquiry became qualitatively quite distinct from the methods used to investigate natural phenomena. Questions of cause and effect gave way to questions of intention, meaning and authorship; for to describe a series of interstellar radio pulses as a message is not to offer an alternative astronomical explanation, it is to offer a *totally different kind* of explanation. The inexorable world of physical processes is replaced by the capricious symbolic world of consciousness. It is not that the physical processes cease or become unimportant, it is that one seeks understanding in a different way. The manner in which the environment is integrated takes on a different pattern.

The Communication Schema

It is at this point that we can bring in usefully the notion of schema. Initially the scientists were applying a schema developed for understanding natural phenomena, but the regularity of the pulses was inconsistent with this schema — that is to say, it conflicted with their expectations. One way of resolving the inconsistency was to switch to a schema that was consistent with the information, namely, to regard the pulses as artificial. Once that transition was made the question was not what caused the pulses, but what purposes they served, and for whom or what.

I would argue that it is this general schema that defines the act of communication and which poses the question of authorship and purpose. It is important to realise that neither author nor purpose need actually exist for the schema to be triggered. It only requires that such a notion be consistent with the available information. In other words, both the author and the purpose are *inferred*. One can take these inferences as a minimal condition for invoking the general communication schema. The inference of authorship is not simply about the existence of an author. That would only allow one to make the natural/artificial distinction without actually saying what purpose the artefact served. The inference is much richer and involves minimally the second assumption that the purpose of the artefact is communication. Notice how Hewish elaborates the inference by the phrase 'another civilization'. It is arguable that an inference could not actually get much richer than that!

Inference and Visual Communication

It is clear that a potential interstellar message must provoke a whole string of speculations about its authorship. At the point of reception there is only the audience/message relation, out of which the author is in a conceptual sense generated. It is as if the message were a garment and we try to deduce the shape and character of the wearer from a study of the clothes.

However, what may be true of an interstellar message may be of little consequence for an understanding of the terrestrial phenomenon, except in this one regard — whenever the author of a message is not immediately present and not intimately known to us there is *always* an element of inference. We must always deduce the form and substance of the author from the cloak of the message. It is because the physical form of the message can exist independently of the author or the audience that visual communication is both important and problematic. It is important because its physical form can outlast the lifetime of many generations and thus provides the basis for a cumulative cultural heritage as each generation can add to the stock of human experience. It is problematic because each generation must regenerate its conception of the author in order to understand the message, and in so doing redefines anew what the message means. It is always tempting to think that the physical form of the message alone constitutes the basis of its meaning and this has led to the misleading practice of analysing the message independently of the author or the audience. The message may be *physically* a distinct entity but the mere fact of calling it a message makes it analytically inseparable from either the author or the audience. The only analytic separation possible is between the audience/message relation on the one hand and the author/message relation on the other. All the forms of communication including visual communication have this in common and therefore there is always an inference which links the audience to the author. So far we have indicated the way in which the audience 'shapes' the author from the fabric of the message as part of our generalised schema for communication.

Communication and Information

It is clear in the case of the potential interstellar message that there is a need to characterise the differences between the pulses as message and the pulses as natural phenomena. It is useful in forming this distinction first to bear in mind that it is not the potential message itself which provides the basis for the distinction but the audience/message relation, and secondly it is worth emphasising at this point that any distinction so formed marks the boundary between what may be regarded as communication and what may not be so regarded. With these points in mind it becomes obvious that to describe something as communication is to say that a particular kind of schema is being applied to it. Thus the locus of definition shifts from the object itself to the relation between that object and its user. In a sense one can describe the schema as a particular set of questions which are used by the audience to interrogate the environment, and only when these questions are asked can we describe the process as communication with respect to the audience/message relation. As we have seen there is a transition between conferring communication status on an aspect of the environment and regarding it as non-communication, and this is characterised by a shift in the questions which are asked of it. Every aspect of the environment may be regarded as a source of *information* but only those aspects which are subjected to the kind of interrogation which has been described above will be defined as *communication*. There is a clear implication from this that not all things which were intended as messages will be seen as such, and equally there will be cases where information from the environment is mistakenly construed as a message.

The Case of the Wink/Twitch

Suppose yourself to be engaged in conversation with someone who, every time he finished a statement, closed and then opened one of his eyes, just once, very quickly. If you took this swift occlusion of the eyelid to be a wink you might be led into thinking that it was an attempt on the part of the speaker to cast humorous doubt on the veracity of his own words. If, however, the thought came to you that here was an unfortunate involuntary recurrent neurological spasm — a twitch — you would do your best to ignore it. (Unless you were a neurologist, when you might do your best to ignore the conversation.) It is clear that only the first of these 'readings' can be regarded as communication from the point of view of the audience/message relation. The other may be regarded only as information. It is also clear that we cannot call the closing of the eyelid a twitch or a wink without prejudging its status in a relation which in itself it does not control.

Within recent years psychologists and ethologists have joined forces in the study of what has come to be known as non-verbal or bodily communication. However, the name is misleading because many of the phenomena being investigated, such as posture and facial expression, are as likely as not to be involuntary; and although a great deal can be learnt from the information that a particular gesture provides about its producer, whether it is thought to have been produced voluntarily or not will significantly affect how one treats it. There is of course a grey area where intentions are not explicit or may even be unconscious. What matters in their reading however is not what they are but what they seem to be and it is certainly the case that not all gestures seem to be communication though they might be very informative.

This crucial difference beween communication and information can be seen clearly in the following situation. Suppose we were examining Figure 6 in the context of a study of the craft of paving; we might reasonably suppose that the intention of the photographer was to show a particular pattern of cobble-stones. But what about the car in the top right-hand corner? It might be that the photographer simply did not notice it when he took the photograph, or that he noticed it but found it impossible to exclude. Or perhaps he deliberately included it to make an ironic comment on the juxtaposition of the old and the new, possibly to show how they negate each other because of the mutual capacity of each for destroying the other. Much more could be read into this single instance of visual communication, and each reading accords different status to the various parts of the image. The information/communication distinction can be seen at work through the changing patterns of meaning that are attributed to the image. If we are to guide people in the use of visual communication we must be

aware of the subtle transformations that can occur in the audience/
message relation and the differentiation between communication and
information is a necessary first step in generating that awareness.

Figure 6

Meaning

Once again I turn to those regular radio signals discussed earlier. It is
now clear how the status of the information reaching the astronomers
was radically transformed by the questions within the communication
schema. The physical phenomenon was no longer present in its own
right as the mere consequence of the operation of physical laws but
was now endowed with a representative function. It stood for
something which was not immediately present and instead of asking:
what is it? and what caused it? the question now being asked was: what
does it mean? This introduces the more general nature of meaning.
We normally ask: what does it mean? when it would be more accurate
to ask: with what meaning can we endow this message? But the form in
which the question is put is significant for two reasons. First, we
assume that anything describable as a message is constructed
according to a set of rules — a code — and when asking questions

about meaning one is appealing to a set of rules either known or supposed. Secondly, it is a way of objectifying knowledge and expectations. Objects 'have' meaning because they have been endowed with it either by individuals or (more usually) by society via a shared code. In other words, meaning is a relation between object and code, not a property of the object itself. An object's meaning may alter by a change in the code, and it is therefore misleading to ask what meaning the object has in the same way that one might ask what colour, or shape, or other physical characteristic it has.

The interstellar radio signal provides some insight into the limits which the object poses on the range of meanings it can be given. In the simplest case one could regard the signal as a bold indicator of the presence of intelligence — artificially produced energy. A second possibility would be to regard the time interval between peaks and troughs as an indicator of some basic important time-span or rhythm in the life of the alien 'civilization'. Thus the first possibility becomes overlaid with a richer meaning, but in either case the signal remains the same. What alters is the code which is applied. Therefore the meaning is not some irreducible property of the signal but is a consequence of the interaction of the signal with a code. It should be clear that there is a limit to the variability within a code that could be matched against a signal. Differences in meaning consistent with the code must match, in however arbitrary a fashion, some discernible differences in the physical energy of the signal.

'What is the Meaning of This Message?'

The true locus of meaning, and its importance in any discussion of communication, will be emphasised continually in this text. Meaning is a *relational* term, not a property of an object. However, it is the case that everyday language suggests otherwise. 'What is the meaning of this message?' is a perfectly legitimate grammatical construction but it does imply that the locus for meaning is in the object. Why should it do so? Why should the normal way in which we ask questions about meaning implicitly objectify the answer? The reason for this is fundamental to an understanding of the social nature of communication. Objectification of meaning provides our social existence with a reality and tangibility it might otherwise lack. This apparent objectivity, when shared, assumes an independence from the individual member of the society. The independent social reality then in turn provides the framework for the social definition of the individual.

Thus the question 'What is the meaning of this message?' is at one and the same time an acknowledgement of an independent social reality and a reinforcement of the position of the individual within that society. What seems to be an innocent construction within our language provides a glimpse of a powerful process in the shaping of individual identity.

A Note on Effects

There is a long tradition of communication research which has focused on the so-called effects of communication. Beginning as an interest in the effects of the mass media (Hovland *et al.*, 1949) it quickly spawned investigations in many areas and the methods of this research have been a mainstay of enquiry in educational technology studies. The presumption behind much of this research has been that studying communication is essentially no different from studying other natural processes and one can look forward with confidence to discovering the cause/effect relations which operate.

That confidence has in the long run been misplaced. In the area of mass communications it has been shown that such effects as are observable are at best marginal (Klapper, 1960) and are certainly a disappointment to expectations. Only in the controlled environment of the laboratory has there been a consistent demonstration of effects but there is widespread scepticism as to the extent that these findings can be generalised to the world beyond.

There is, however, one seemingly controlled environment which has lent itself to many studies of communication effect — the classroom. Here the picture is clear. There has been no shortage of demonstrations of 'effect' but:

> During the last few decades we have frittered away an enormous amount of research time asking relatively useless questions about the media of instruction. *Can the media teach?* has been asked over and over again, and over and over again the answer has come back: *of course*, students can learn effectively from the media, from *any* medium. *Can they teach as well as a teacher?* The answer: what they can do, they can do as well as a classroom teacher, sometimes better. It depends on the performance of the teacher, the content of the media, what is being taught, and to whom. *Is one*

medium any more effective than others? For some purposes, probably yes, but overall there is no superlative medium of instruction, any more than there is one simple algorithm for selecting one medium over others. We have come to realize in recent decades that learning from the media is not an area that lends itself to simple answers. (Schramm, 1977, p. 14)

However, even this indictment misses the main, central mistake in the search for effects, and the conclusion that the process is complex and multivariate merely suggests that we become more sophisticated at doing the same thing. I would argue an end to all studies of this kind, however cleverly contrived, because communication is not understandable in these terms (Sless, 1978). The transition from the realm of cause and effect to that of meaning is not an increase in complexity. It is a fundamental difference in quality. To talk about the effects of a message is to presume that the message has an existence independent of the other aspects of the communication process, that is, it can be treated as an independent variable in an experimental procedure; but as I have already argued in this text we shall treat the audience/ message and author/message as the units of analysis and at no time will the message itself be treated as a separate entity. This marks an important break between the tradition of enquiry in this area and this work.

Behaviourism and Rules

Readers familiar with modern linguistics will recognise elements of the evaluation of studies of effect, given above, as part of the classic critique of behaviourism by Chomsky (Chomsky, 1959). In fairness to behaviourists there have been some spirited defences of behaviourism (MacCorquodale, 1970) which successfully rebuff all but one of the criticisms, but that a major one, being the inability of behaviourism to deal with the problem of selective attention. Simply, it is the problem of explaining how an organism attends to one thing rather than another. While selective attention is a feature of both human and animal behaviour, behaviourism has been incapable of providing an adequate explanation despite numerous attempts to do so. This basic inadequacy is not due to a lack of theoretical ingenuity, but to behaviourism's fundamental theoretical presupposition, which is that the stimulus impinging on the organism is the prime determinant of behaviour; and any explanation of how we select (along with all other activities) must issue from the supposed primacy of the stimulus. The impossibility of accommodating within the theory such an active process as attention strikes at the very heart of the behaviourist approach in all its many forms.

However, if one adopts the notion of schema as developed here then the problem of selective attention disappears. As Neisser suggests, 'When perception is treated as something we do rather than as something thrust upon us, no internal mechanisms of selection are required at all' (Neisser, 1976, p. 84). To account for what happens in terms of action rather than in terms of response to stimuli is a definite shift in perspective, one which simply rejects the fundamental assumptions of behaviourism and hence the study of effects whether of communication or of any other process which is part of a non-mechanical system. It is this which would make meaningless any question of effects in relation to the pulsar signal. But we must still confront the question of what it is that guides the individual's action, and this is where we must try to describe the schemata which control action. Here again anyone familiar with modern linguistics will recognise the importance given in that field to the study of the rules which govern language behaviour. There are many features which visual communication shares with language and I will be pointing to these in later chapters. However, many of the rules governing visual communication are not only quite different to linguistic rules but, moreover, they do not necessarily enjoy the high degree of cultural uniformity present in language. It would be very misleading to presume that the rules governing the audience/message relation can be specified with anything approaching the precision used in linguistics, and one should bear in mind that most of the theoretical findings in modern linguistics have been achieved by idealising the language process rather than by being concerned with specific language acts. (Chomsky's distinction between performance and competence, and de Saussure's distinction between *la langue* and *parole* make this quite clear (Chomsky, 1965; de Saussure, 1974).)

Notwithstanding these considerations, it is in terms of rules, and not in terms of cause and effect, that we shall be looking for an understanding of visual communication.

Postscript to the Pulsar

The case of the pulsating radio waves, which we have been studying throughout this chapter, has been very instructive, precisely because it is marginal. After their discovery, radio telescopes all over the world searched the sky for similar sources, and in due course more were found. Armed with more data the scientific community settled down to the task of unravelling the mystery of the new phenomena; the physical explanation prevailed, and they came to be known as pulsars, short for 'pulsating stars'. Now, it is quite clear that any future candidate for the title of potential interstellar message will have to show more than mere regularity to trigger the communication schema of the scientific community. It would however seem to take very little to provoke some writers to overexercise their communication schemata in pursuit of the alien message. Any analysis of such attempts would do well to look to the motivations of the writer and his devoted readers than at the effect of the messages! The fact that many of these so-called messages take a visual form should not however go unnoticed, and anyone interested in the way objectification can dominate reasoning would find these chariots of fancy very interesting.

The Author/Message Relation

As the uncluttered quality of the last example served us so well in affording a glimpse of the underlying schema of the audience, I propose to keep the cosmic connection open to help us focus on the second of the relations discussed earlier, the author/message relation.

Two messages have been deliberately constructed and sent into space (see Figures 7 and 8). Because they both take a visual form, I will use them to extend this general discussion of communication into a discussion of visual communication.

Initially I want to penetrate the assumptions governing the construction of the messages and for this purpose I will concentrate on the Arecibo message, though all the general points apply equally to both.

The Inferred Audience

In communication with each other we take so much for granted about what we believe lies in common between us, that it is very difficult to expose the hidden form of presuppositions which not only shapes our construction of messages but in doing so indirectly offers a mantle

Figure 7: The Arecibo Message of 1974

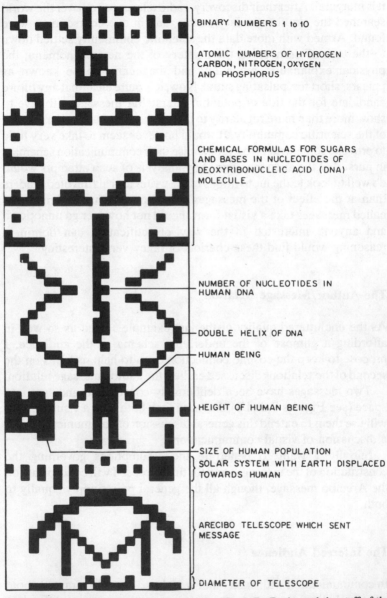

Source: The Arecibo Message is designed by Frank D. Drake and the staff of the National Astronomy and Ionosphere Center. The Arecibo Observatory is part of the National Astronomy and Ionosphere Center which is operated by Cornell University under contract with the National Science Foundation.

Figure 8: The Pioneer Plaque

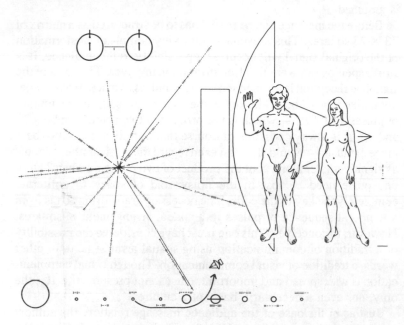

Source: With permission of Carl Sagan.

shaped to fit what we believe to be the nature of our audience. This makes the Arecibo message and the Pioneer plaque valuable aids to understanding, because we can have no knowledge of the audience for these messages and any assumptions that were made when they were constructed can be revealed in a way impossible with earthbound communication.

The Arecibo message, so called because the giant Arecibo radio telescope was used as the transmitter, was beamed out as a set of 1,679 pulses towards the Great Cluster in Hercules in 1974.

The most obvious presupposition which gives shape to the inferred audience is that it must have a radio receiver and some means of memorising or recording the message. This in turn involves the presumption that the audience might be monitoring the radio frequencies and most important, as a prerequisite, would be capable of making the distinction between natural and aritifical energy emission, which as we saw in the case of the pulsars was at the basis of the suspicion that the regular signal might have been a message for us.

Thus the abilty to distinguish between information and communication is assumed.

Before the message can be read it has to be structured as a matrix of 73×23 squares. This presumes that a very complex transformation of the original signal will occur as a possibility to the audience. It is worth spelling out what this transformation involves. The form of the signal on reception is a single sequence of pulses over a period of time, not unlike morse code. The key to the code at this stage is the number of pulses — 1,679 — which is the product of two prime numbers 73 and 23. It is always possible of course that our alien takes it to be a piece of music — would she then even regard the total number of notes as significant, let alone spot the product of two prime numbers? Only one pulse need be lost in the noisy void of space to obliterate completely the key to the code. The necessary transformation is from a temporal sequence of pulses to a spatial arrangement of squares. However, to conceive of this one must have considered the possibility of a tradition of communication using spatial arrangement, in other words, a tradition of visual communication. Though visual communication is widespread and important, one cannot presume that it is the only, nor even a necessary, basis of a culture.

Just as in the case of the audience/message relation, the author/ message relation provides a cloak for the absent other. It is as if the message were a suit tailored to the presumed measurements of the audience. In this example it is very clear that the character of the audience is a guess. It could not be other than an intelligent hunch about the likely evolution of life in another environment. What is also very clear is that it is logically impossible to construct *any* message without at the same time constructing the absent audience.

Knowledge of the Audience

It might be tempting to suggest that the peculiar problems of communicating with an unknown alien are very different from communication within our own species and within our own culture. The logical imperative to construct the audience would on the face of it be easier to comply with if one knew the audience at first hand. However, knowledge of the audience at first hand cannot be assumed and even where present, translating that knowledge into a sensitively structured message is a great art.

Consider all the possibilities for misunderstanding which are a

natural consequence of face-to-face communication between individuals. To these add the misunderstanding which might arise from
indirect forms of communication, such as visual communication; and
take this one stage further to the mass produced communication of the
mass media where it becomes apparent that there is an even greater
possibility for misunderstanding.

It is instructive to look at studies of mass media communicators
and discover how they go about acquiring knowlege of their audience
in order to respond to the logical imperative to construct the inferred
audience. The general finding is that they are woefully ignorant of
their audience (Golding, 1974; Schlesinger, 1978). The reasons for
this are both structural and traditional. First, the organisational
structure of mass media production is not geared to respond sensitively
to its audience. The only consistent information available directly
from the audience is in the form of ratings, which merely informs
potential advertisers or sponsors about the number of potential
consumers the station, network or newspaper can deliver. It says
nothing about their interest in, comprehension of, or learning from a
particular form. Secondly, and in the long run more importantly, it is
not part of the traditional skills in any of these areas to investigate the
audience or its comprehension of material. Only in certain specialised
areas of education and advertising is there some structural commitment to understanding and evaluation but the traditions of practice
from which these arise are psychology, educational testing, social
science and statistics, not art, design, literature or film and television
production. The conflict in practice which arises at the meeting point
of these disparate traditions will be well known to anyone who has had
to mediate between them. In advertising there is a constant tension
between creative and research departments. In education similar
conflicts arise. Educational technology units are often dominated by
educational evaluators rather than media producers. This is reflected
both in the formal quality of the output and the emphasis on quasi-
scientific evaluation. It is clear from a recent review that there is now
some doubt whether such units have lived up to their promise
(Schramm, 1977). Equally there is no evidence that the professionally
produced media product is more effective for being so produced.

There are exceptions and I will be turning towards these later. The
point I wish to make now is that in most of the instances of visual
communication that we are likely to come across, the author's
knowledge of the audience cannot be assumed, but some conception
of that audience, however derived, is a necessary prerequisite in the

construction of messages; the concept of the inferred audience is a valuable pointer to an undertanding of the author/message relation. The inferred audience is occasionally a sensitive guide, in the construction of messages, but more often than not it is a stereotyped thumbnail sketch which serves as a minimal frame for the author's purpose. Nor is the label of professionalism an assurance of effectiveness despite the fact that, as Schlesinger has found, professionals '... assert their possession of the necessary knowledge for effective communication'. He goes on to say:

> When pressed they produce vague ideas about their audience, based on their view of the kinds of people who listen to or watch particular channels, or from interactions with neighbours or people on trains. Ultimately the newsman is his own audience. When he talks of his professionalism he is saying that he knows how to tell his story. (Schlesinger, 1978, p. 134)

These comments are based on a study of the producers of BBC television news, one of the most prestigious communication institutions. It is possible to see how the tradition of practice in news-gathering, in common with all the other communicating arts, does not include a continuing investigation of the audience.

The historical reason for this is that all of these arts grew out of smaller and more homogeneous cultural environments where the author and the audience were very close and could truly be said to know one another. The forms of practice and excellence which provide today's practitioners with their skills and critical standards are still based on these notions, but are operating in a mass-produced form serving a heterogeneous culture to which the practitioners have a limited, uninformed and inappropriate access.

It is therefore necessary to exercise extreme care when discussing the so-called 'power of the media'. Like magic in primitive societies, its ability to work is less significant in the long run than the belief in its efficacy and more importantly, the belief in the institutions of practice that it maintains. In human societies of all kinds, there is a long tradition of belief in the possibility of direct power over individuals by indirect means. Religion, magic and the mass media have all laid claim to such powers at some time and their survival as institutions has never depended on the proof of their claims. In a very important sense their claims to power are not false because in each case they are woven into the structure of the society in such a way that it is impossible to understand these societies, and the behaviour of the individuals within them, without taking the power of these institutions very seriously (Evans-Pritchard, 1937). One does not have to try proving the efectiveness of prayer in order to explain the power of religion.

Not surprisingly the 'power of the media' has strongly influenced education. At the level of policy and hence the purse that 'power' has been very potent; at the level of message-making the educational technology cauldron has not produced an irresistible teaching potion despite the incantation of educational objectives, media selection, evaluation and testing.

The belief in the power of messages over an audience is an aspect of the constructed inferred audience. It does not follow that the actual audience will behave in the way anticipated. There is a complex network of possibilities which is only partly circumscribed by the form and content of the message, which is one of the reasons why the analysis of the message on its own in some kind of imagined neutral space is of little value.

The Arecibo message and the Pioneer plaque are full of presumptions about their audience. This is obvious. It is less so when dealing with human communications. But it is always worth bearing in mind that whereas there is a logical imperative to construct the audience in the author/message relation, there is no logical imperative, nor is there even a tradition of practice, that such a construction has to be based on a detailed or sensitive knowledge of an actual audience.

Equally as we discovered no such restraint operates in the audience/message relation where the inferred author is also a construction.

This is the basic framework from which I will proceed to a detailed analysis of visual communication. It is a way of dealing with the uncertainty of the communication process but at the same time probing its regularities. It may seem that this is a circuitous route towards the pedagogic uses of visual material. However, education is parasitic on the modes of communication available in our culture and it is from this more general perspective that we need to understand visual communication.

3 VISUAL COMMUNICATION — THE AUTHOR/ MESSAGE RELATION

Introduction

We take many things for granted. We presume that if someone has had adequate professional training and experience as a communicator, be it journalist, typographer, graphic designer, illustrator, photographer or film or television producer, that he has the necessary skills to construct effective communication. I want to explore this belief both generally and as it affects education. There are, as we shall discover, good reasons, indeed there is compelling evidence, to suggest that this assumption is questionable; it will emerge from this that professional practice is prey to a number of typical errors of judgement which can powerfully reduce the educational value of any material produced.

Throughout this chapter we will be concerned with the author/ message relation. It will of necessity be an abbreviated account but it will be drawing on a wide range of material. There is more than one level at which the relations between author and message can be examined. There is always some institutional framework guiding practice: broadcasting station, advertising agency, production company, community of scholars, publishing house or audio-visual unit. The social organisation of these institutions provides the basic working environment for the professional communicators and determines the basic goals and purposes of practice. A further level at which we can examine the process of communication is in terms of the ethics or value system which professionals claim to abide by. This generally covers what those in the professions would consider a proper or improper use of their talents. Moving into any specific area — say graphic design, photography or journalism — we find traditions of practice. These traditions, the accumulated wisdom of sometimes centuries of practitioners, which are passed on either through formal or informal training or apprenticeship, become the body of skills which we most clearly identify as the hallmark of the professional.

It is the interpenetration of all these that provides an understanding of the author/message relation: a combination of craft, institution and ethics. Just how these function together towards effective communication will be the subject of this chapter.

Effective Communication — the Primary Focus

Effectiveness, as I have commented elsewhere (Sless, 1978) is one of those contemporary words which paralyses thought but gives the illusion that one is racing along towards an understanding of the communication process. It is not unusual in everyday conversation to hear the phrase 'How very effective!' being used as part of someone's critical vocabulary about a painting, a poster, a television programme or any piece of communication, but what does it mean? More specifically, in what sense will it be used here? If our discussion of the author/message relation is going to focus around this question, 'effectiveness' must be carefully defined. In Chapter 2, I dismissed the use of the mechanistic notion of effects in the study of communication as inappropriate but that is certainly one of the senses in which the word is commonly used. There is another more convoluted sense which often arises when judging the likely consequences of a message on others, as when we might say of an advertisement, a party political broadcast or even a school's textbook, that it is very effective, yet at the same time not buy the product, change one's opinion or remember the information in the book. In this case one may be saying that although one is not the kind of person who normally responds to advertising by buying the product, is not persuaded by political rhetoric into changing one's opinion, does not need that kind of presentation to absorb information, none the less people 'out there', the 'masses', 'ordinary people' or 'children' will find the message irresistible. (It is also possible that one is simply saying that the message is in a very general way memorable, but this possibility I take to be trivial.) This sense of 'effective' has serious connotations.

It stems from two misconceptions. First, it presumes that one's own position is in a curious sense neutral when in fact it is not. The moralist who takes it upon himself to hunt out immorality, the ideologue who searches for implicit propaganda, the critic who tells us what we should like and the educator who decides by what instruments we should learn, all proceed from a position of some commitment. Secondly, it is not possible for the moralist, ideologue, critic or educator to decide on the basis of an analysis of the message alone what will happen in the audience/message relation. At the very least the audience component of that relation is a construction. It is a presumed entity vaguely characterised by terms such as 'the masses', 'other people' or 'children' all of which tells us a great deal about the person conducting the analysis of the message but can hardly be taken seriously as an accurate and sensitive understanding of the audience it purports to describe. It does, however, provide us with yet another compelling reason why the analysis of the message in a presumed neutral space is misleading and inevitably involves a conflation of the audience/message relation if not also the author/message relation.

'Effectiveness' as used in this book will not refer to any of the above senses. It will be concerned with the ability of the author within the author/message relation to be able to foresee and describe accurately the audience/message relation. Obviously a great deal will depend on the instrumentalities and procedures available within the author/ message relation for acquiring knowledge of the audience, and therefore the question of effectiveness will largely focus on these aspects of professional communications which deal with the inferred audience, an integral part in the construction of any message.

The Institutional Framework

The study of the institutions surrounding the activity of professional communicators, particularly those working in the mass media, has been a very fruitful area of sociological research and from the accumulated findings of many studies it is possible to map out the general features of such institutions as they relate to the effectiveness of communication (Blumler, 1969; Burns, 1969; Elliott, 1972; Gans, 1979; Golding and Elliott, 1976).

It is a defining characteristic of the mass media that the author is structurally separated from the audience; a small relatively isolated group (the author) produces messages for a large undifferentiated anonymous audience. This is as true of BBC news as it is of a textbook in physics or psychology. The very technology which makes such large-scale communication possible is by its nature basically insensitive to the needs of its audience. But, as I pointed out in Chapter 2, there is a logical imperative to construct the audience; it is necessary to ask how institutions respond to this logical imperative. A more familiar formulation of this question enquires into the way that organisations concerned with communication are structured in order to provide the professional communicator with knowledge of the audience. There are two formal ways in which organisations do respond to the imperative. The first and in many ways most obvious is in the provision of an audience research department or unit. The second is more difficult to point to but is, as we shall see, more important — I will describe it as the surrogate audience. Audience research is, in the history of communication, a relative newcomer frequently treated as an interloper. It has grown out of the combined skills of social science survey techniques, psychological testing, demography and statistics. Most of the large organisations of mass communication either conduct their own research or contract out. Smaller organisations such as advertising agencies or publishing houses tend to use the services of specialist market research companies that undertake audience research. In educational establishments, where the scale of operations is very much smaller, it is not unusual to have someone with a knowledge of educational testing actually in charge of an audio-visual production unit. However, it would be very misleading to suggest that audience research actually helps towards effective communication, though there can be little doubt that the organisations in question do believe it to fulfil that purpose. I shall examine this point more fully when we examine the traditions of practice among professional communicators.

The surrogate audience is as it suggests a substitute for the real audience. It is formally represented within organisations by an editor, or director, and informally by a whole network of colleagues, acquaintances, friends and family, inside and outside the organisation. Another powerful source of influence is the client. The advertising agency sells its services to a manufacturer, not to the public. An audio-visual unit 'sells' its services to the teaching staff, not the students. The manufacturer and the teachers are in a sense gate-keepers; without their approval the author is without an audience. In many instances they may well be deemed to be the real audience, with the public or the students coming a poor second.

These, then, are the sources of information available to organisations to enable the author to construct the audience. We must turn to the value systems which operate in these organisations to acquire further insight into the way in which this information is used.

Professionalism and the Inferred Audience

There is no shortage of fine words linking professional communicators to their audience. The newsman's code of impartiality, objectivity and ultimate responsiblity to his audience can be found in the written codes of many professional communicators, so that if one were to take these noble sentiments at their face value one could rest assured that the audience was well cared for. However, the realities of the situation are rather different.

Communications, as we have seen, poses special problems in that the sources of information about effectiveness of performance are all indirect or surrogate. Some workers can easily point to the material and tangible products of their craft: a bricklayer can point to a wall, a dentist to the fillings, an engineer to a bridge. The communicator cannot do so as readily. Even in the areas of advertising or political propaganda, where sales or votes would seem to offer indices of success, so many additional factors can intervene between messages and ultimate behaviour at the supermarket or polling booth that effective communication is virtually beyond evaluation in these areas. This is not how the advertising industry would explain how it functions — but it is significant that the evidence offered by advertisers to potential clients as an indication of their effectiveness rarely consists of a detailed breakdown of their campaign record; more typically it consists of a list of their clients and their annual turnover. Thus the size and prestige of the client becomes an indication of the effectiveness of the agency. The real problem of the advertising industry is to maintain its credibility, and there are many ways of achieving that end without answering the ultimate question: does it work?

The audience, however, despite its inaccessibility, will not go away; there persists the logical imperative to construct the audience within the message. This problem faces all professional communicators but what emerges from the research is that various aspects of the professional value system protect members from direct confrontation with the issue. This has the effect of displacing audience research and placing the emphasis on what I have described as the surrogate audience. McQuail (1969) identified four characteristic ways in which communicators, as authors, negotiate the uncertainty generated by this ignorance of the audience: paternalism, specialisation, professionalism and ritualism. Paternalism is simply the assumption that one does not need to know the audience to know what is right for it — a familiar enough posture in all the communicating arts, not excluding education. Specialisation is the narrowing down of the communication task to the immediate programme or message. Professionalism, which is used in a more restricted sense by McQuail than I use it here, is the employment of a professional code, such as the newsman's notion of 'objectivity' or the graphic designer's use of 'aesthetic criteria', as a basis for judgement. Finally ritualism is the

application of techniques or methods which are believed to have
worked in the past. Most obviously this method can be observed in the
hunt for ratings which television networks indulge in. If a programme
or series has been successful (that is, attracts large audiences), we are
subjected to more of the same or similar until the ratings begin to drop.
Ratings are a special exception in the audience research category.
Their economic importance is crucial. They enable the network to sell
an audience to an advertiser. The bigger the audience, the bigger the
potential market, the higher the cost of the time and hence the greater
the revenue of the network. But the ratings figure is only a body count.
It does not tell the professional why a particular programme was or
was not watched.

Ritualism has a much wider and more subtle dimension covering
the whole range of techniques and conventions which guide professional
practice; these will be dealt with more fully in a later section.

The above findings are based on studies of communicators working
in the mass media. The extent to which they can be generalised to
other contexts — say the working of an audio-visual department in a
college or university — must be treated with some reservations; but it
is legitimate to ask what level of direct contact exists or is possible
between those who make the messages and those for whom they are
intended, and I do not mean the indirect contact of a lecturer or tutor
who may be in a certain important sense quite remote from the
students. The point of central importance is that if there is any
uncertainty about the audience/message relation, the tendency is for
it to be resolved, and any gap filled, by reference to the surrogate
audience rather than by appeal to the real audience.

It might be thought that what I have described is a very self-
conscious process. This is not the case. As Schlesinger puts it in his
study of BBC news-making:

> You do not find people wandering around in a state of existential
> *Angst* wondering whether they are 'communicating' or not. You do
> on the other hand, find an intense obsession with the packaging of
> the broadcast, and comparative evaluation of others' goods.
> (Schlesinger, 1978, p. 107)

There is thus an inclination towards hermeticism, but that is not the
sole reason why audience research has not played a larger role in the
author/message relation. To clarify the issue further, we must now
take a closer look at the traditions of practice of the professional

communicator which is the extension and elaboration of ritualism into the making of messages.

Traditions of Practice

All the traditions of practice we commonly associate with contemporary communication grew out of preindustrial society. While this is obvious in such cases as literature, graphic design or illustration, it is not so obvious in the case of radio, film and television, but these all have their roots in literature, drama and music, all of which pre-date the earliest mass-produced forms — the printed word and image. The preindustrial author could claim with some justification that he knew his audience. It was against the rough edge of that knowledge that he honed and sharpened his skill. Societies, small by present-day standards, were in the case of writers very small, since literacy was not universal; and even painters and sculptors were working for an audience that was potentially knowable. They were in a very real sense part of the same society as their audience. There was therefore no need for them to acquire any special skills in order to understand the audience/message relation, for they participated in that relation as a matter of course. All the skills lay in the execution of the work. Despite the changed milieu it is still the case that a training in any of the contemporary communicative arts is a training in execution, with no attention given to the skills that would be useful in order to develop a knowledge of the audience/message relation.

A further link with the preindustrial and prescientific origins of communication practice is what might be described as a craft-based epistemology. Communication is learnt as a craft which means that knowledge is practical, increases in sophistication with practice and is often tacit and unrecorded. Thus there is an emphasis on working experience and intuition as the basis of professional judgement and this provides us with an insight into the reasons why audience research has remained a relatively minor aspect of professional practice. The subjects out of which audience research have grown have tended to have their ideological roots in positivism, that is the belief that only scientifically derived findings may be considered true knowledge. Clearly this represents a complete contrast and a sharp challenge to the craft-based knowledge of the practitioners. Very simply there is no meeting point. The communicator has been schooled to trust his own judgement and that of his mentors and peers, the audience researcher has been trained only to accept as true that which is determined by a controlled experiment or survey. This is at the basis of the mutual incomprehension and hostility which is often found within organisations where these two functions try to work towards the common goal of effective communication. This, along with the aspects of professional life already discussed, keeps the author/message relation isolated and tending towards hermeticism, what one researcher described as a situation of 'autistic activity and belief' (Burns, 1969, p.70).

It would be true to say of most professional communicators that they are ignorant of their audience and have neither the skills nor the inclination to dispel that ignorance. This, however, does not mean that they are not effective communicators. For one thing it is probably the case that tacit knowledge is very important and a lifetime considering alternative solutions to practical problems of communication does provide an insight into the most likely solutions, and for another, any author, however remote from the audience, is still within the same society and is likely to draw on conventions that he believes are shared by his audience. He is likely to be partially successful some of the time. What lies tantalisingly out of reach is knowing when, how and with whom.

Visual Communication Practice: The Legacy of the Bauhaus

The account so far has been very generalised and has focused on the social circumstances which provide the backdrop against which the author/message relation works. I want to look now specifically at the practices which most closely bear on the subject of this book. The range of professions which could be said to be within the sphere of visual communication is vast and there are a number of ways in which they can be traditionally grouped. The most obvious grouping is probably in terms of medium; thus one can discern typography, photography, painting, sculpture, film-making, etc. While these still exist as accepted professions their boundaries are very loose — the typographer is likely to use a whole range of specialist photographic techniques, any of the others would on occasion make use of skills more closely identified with another medium of specialisation. Another kind of division is in terms of subject, so one can talk about cartography, medical illustration, advertising and so on. Each of these may cut across traditional media boundaries but put these media to work in relatively specialist subject areas. It is therefore impossible to generalise, even to say that they share a common heritage of techniques and attitudes.

There is however one source of inspiration which has played an important role in the stylistic development of visual communications in the twentieth century: the Bauhaus Basic Design Course. While it is neither the only nor necessarily the most worthwhile influence, it has the distinguishing characteristic of providing a coherent pedagogic programme based on what looks like a scientific basis, and most importantly it is used as the basic introductory course in most colleges of art. As it is through these institutions that many professional visual communicators acquire their initial training, the Bauhaus Basic Design Course can be seen as an important substratum to a great many assumptions and practices in contemporary visual communication.

The Bauhaus was a school of design set up in 1919 in Dessau, Germany, by the architect Walter Gropius. It attracted among its teaching staff and students some of the most distinguished artists and designers of the period. It is probably best known for its development of the style of industrial and architectural design known as Functionalism, but the Basic Design Course, which provided the formal basis for Functionalism and remains a persistent influence, is probably less well known. Many art educators in primary, secondary and tertiary education use elements of the course without realising their origin.

The Basic Design Course consists of a series of practical exercises which students perform under supervision. They are designed to reveal progressively how images are constructed out of a number of basic elements such as point, line, texture and colour. As there are an infinite variety of ways in which these elements can be used both in realistic images and in pattern-making, there is no limit to the number of exercises which students can perform. There is therefore even within such a tight formal programme considerable scope for individual differences and ingenuity. The progressive revelation of the basic elements is accompanied by an intense preoccupation with different materials for image-making and a great deal of stress is placed on using materials in a manner which does not abuse the quality of these materials, and which (it is hoped) celebrates their peculiar characteristics. Finally there is important emphasis placed on the way in which elements interact with each other and the space they occupy. Many exercises are directed at developing the students' awareness of these three factors: elements, materials and interaction. If, for the purposes of this brief account, I had to translate it into a practical picture-making context I could say very simply that the Basic Design Course was intended to equip the student with the ability to answer three kinds of questions: What elements (lines, points, etc.) should I use to construct my picture; what materials (felt tip, paint, etc.) would be most suited to the task; and how should I organise the various parts of the picture with respect to one another within the picture frame? The same questions could be asked with respect to the printed page, poster, sculpture — for that matter any visible experience an artist wanted to create. This generalisable quality of the Basic Design Course has given it very wide appeal among educators in the field of art and design.

The main architects of the Basic Design Course were the artists Klee, Kandinsky, Moholy-Nagy, Itten and Albers. Much of their thinking and teaching is still widely available and used (Klee, 1972; Moholy-Nagy, 1938; Itten, 1975; Albers, 1975). To understand the climate which led to the development of the Basic Design Course it is necessary to position the Bauhaus historically. It was established at a time when the traditional role of artists and craftsmen was either disappearing or being subjected to radical change. Mechanisation of production meant the gradual demise and loss of the skills of craftsmanship; artists, finding their traditional role threatened by photography, and released from the imperative of realism, had begun to experiment more freely with pictures and the whole concept of picturing.

All of these factors were present at the time of the establishment of the Bauhaus which over the years of its existence gradually developed a response to the new conditions. Its teachers evolved a variety of ways which were not necessarily compatible with or sympathetic to each other, but which led collectively to a rejection of the classic academy education of young artists which at that time consisted of acquiring techniques of representation according to the conventions of realism developed since the Renaissance. In its place they sought a simplification, a purification. 'Every new student arrives encumbered with a mass of accumulated information which he must abandon before he can achieve perception and knowledge that are really his own' (Itten, quoted in Banham, 1960).

The obvious romanticism of this position has always posed problems for the advocates of the Basic Design Course because it implies an emphasis on individual creativity at the expense of social role and a reliance on intuitive judgement rather than the acquisition of knowledge. The purification process was not to be achieved in a vacuum. The students were to be guided through practical exercises to a realisation of the fundamental building blocks of visual experience. Some, like Itten and Klee, believed that this purification had a kind of mystic significance which sat uneasily within the mechanistic era in which they lived. Others, like Moholy-Nagy, saw within it an opportunity to come to terms with the machine age. The simple forms that machines fabricated so easily could be made beautiful by the application of a simplifying aesthetic which responded to the properties of the material. We can see the force of this argument if we examine contemporary designs that owe their origins to this Bauhaus conception (Figure 9). There was, however, agreement that the building blocks of visual experience were in some sense fundamental and were therefore the basis of what they took to be a universal language of visual communication. This belief in universality is of major importance.

Viewed from the central ideas of this book the practical exercises are a systematic procedure for *changing* the schemata of the student from a functional mode developed for purposes of survival, to a formal mode for purposes of message-making; the continual practical performance of tasks consistent with these formal schemata helps to objectify them so that in the end the student's world 'is' composed of point, line, texture and colour in dynamic interaction.

The exponents of the Basic Design Course sought legitimation for their new system in the current theories of their time, and two scientific theories of the day provided the substantive findings and metaphors which sustained the pedagogic practice and the underlying theory: Gestalt theory from psychology and relativity theory from physics.

Gestalt and Basic Design

The Gestalt psychologists had discovered what they claimed to be the laws of visual organisation (Koffka, 1935), two of which are illustrated in Figure 10. The law of similarity (Figure 10a) states that objects which are alike tend to be grouped together. The law of proximity (Figure 10b) states that objects close to one another tend to be grouped together. These simple demonstrations were very persuasive and along with the other laws were eagerly adopted as the scientific basis for the Basic Design Course's theory of image-making. That theory has been repeatedly articulated (Kepes, 1944; de Sausmarez, 1964; Dondis, 1973). Possibly its most articulate

Figure 9

supporter is the art critic Rudolph Arnheim (Arnheim, 1956). If the claim of Gestalt psychology to have discovered fundamental laws of visual organisation were true, an understanding of those laws by anyone wishing to communicate would be invaluable. One would be able to predict how audiences would naturally organise what they saw in pictures and on the printed page, and this knowledge could be used to advantage when designing pictures or the printed page.

. . . the very same means the human organism uses to decode and organise and make sense out of visual information, all information for that matter, could serve most effectively for composing a message to be viewed by an audience. The process of human information input, in its psychological physiological ramifications, could serve as a model for information output. (Dondis, 1973, p. 96)

Figure 10a

O O X X O O X X O O X X O O

Figure 10b

O O   O O   O O   O O   O O

That is, if we understand how messages are decoded then we can efficiently encode them with that knowledge in mind. Notice how this theory of image-making is also a theory of the audience. It is a means of constructing the audience within the author/message relation without direct reference to the audience/message relation itself. Gestalt theory seems to provide an account of the principles which govern the audience/message relation, and hence there is apparently no need to go to the audience. This provided continuity with the craft-based practice of the traditional artist, which I discussed above, while seeming to embrace modern scientific knowledge with its claim to have discovered general laws.

It is this faith in the universality of the underlying processes which led Kepes a generation earlier to declare the universality of visual communications.

The visual language is capable of disseminating knowledge more effectively than almost any other vehicle of communication. With it, man can express and relay his experiences in object form. Visual communication is universal and international: it knows no limits of tongue, vocabulary, or grammar, and it can be perceived by the illiterate as well as the literate. Visual language can convey facts and ideas in a wider and deeper range than almost any other means of communication. (Kepes, 1944, p. 13)

Such rhetoric from a leader in art education was powerfully influential on those within its orbit and the belief in the power of visual material is very persistent. It has led among other things to the use of pictorial symbols for purposes of international communication and the strong advocacy of their use by graphic designers. As it happens, the results of extensive studies of both international symbols and the so-called laws of Gestalt organisation have not revealed the basis of a lingua franca, nor have the many practical studies of the 'language of vision' supported the claim.

Gestalt psychology was an important stage in the development of the modern psychological theory of perception but its claim to have discovered the laws of visual organisation has been taken too literally. 'There are no adequate means for specifying the variables which underlie the organisations predicted by the laws. Thus, the laws appear to be descriptions of perception rather than laws of perception' (Haber and Hershenson, 1974, p. 189). However, it would be wrong to dismiss entirely the value of Gestalt psychology. It was as Gombrich recently reminded us, '. . . the first theory of perception which systematically opposed the "bucket theory" of a passive registration of stimuli' (Gombrich, 1979, p. 4). In doing so it opened the way to a consideration of the organising potential of vision. The Gestalt 'laws' are examples of this and the work of the Bauhaus teachers and their pupils represents a further extension into the fluid and often vague realms of visual communications.

Despite the absence of adequate theory, it is possible to see by way of an example how objectification can sustain the belief that pictorial space is indeed structured in a manner that can provide a seemingly firm foundation for an elaborate set of conventions within visual communication practice.

Figure 11 is taken from Maurice de Sausmarez's book *Basic Design: the Dynamics of Visual Form*, which has been a recommended text for many courses in graphic design in the UK, and has been reprinted continuously since its first publication in 1964. First look carefully at the dots, then read the following, which is part of the caption which accompanies it, and notice how this transforms the experience.

Figure 11

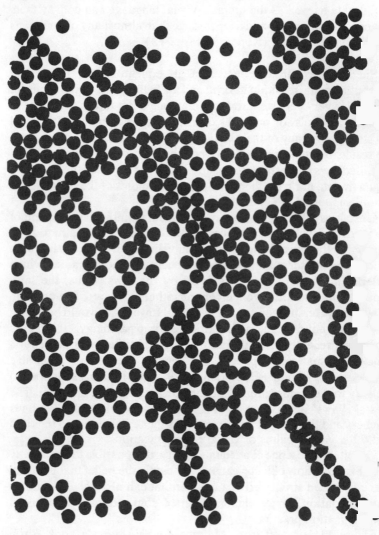

Source: Maurice de Sausmarez, *Basic Design: the Dynamics of Visual Form* (Studio Vista, London, 1964).

. . . a printed dot is directly related to personal imagery. A riot is being quelled by soldiers — each dot symbolises a person and the rioters and the soldiers are only distinguished by the character of the groupings related to the clear spaces. (p. 21)

The passage preceding this illustration and caption provides the 'lawful' context.

The simplest unit, a spot, not only indicates location but is felt to have within itself potential energies of expansion and contraction which activate the surrounding area. When two spots occur there is a statement of measurement and implied direction and the 'inner' energies create a specific tension between them which directly affects the intervening space.

Freely used spots, in clusters or spread out, create a variety of energies and tensions activating the entire area over which they occur.

... A line can be thought of as a chain of spots joined together. It indicates position and direction and has within itself a certain energy; the energy appears to travel along its length and to be intensified at either end, speed is implied and the space around it is activated. (p. 20)

This is part of the preliminary to Figure 11. It is necessary to read such writing, which occurs throughout this literature, with a certain involvement. It would not do to adopt too critical a stance. The reader who does so would find this, and writing similar to it, very irritating. However, the effect on the willing reader is apparent if such a reader looks at Figure 11 with the above firmly in mind.

I have deliberately reversed the order in which the section would normally be approached, to give some sense of the power of objectification in concretising the structuring of the so-called 'visual laws'.

If one accepts the validity of all the points leading to the image then it only has a confirmatory role. It is not unlike the subtle trick practised in texts on linguistics and linguistic philosophy where, after the authors have carefully prepared a suitable context, one discovers that the sentence, 'Our store sells alligator shoes', is actually ambiguous! (Katz and Foder, 1963). There is a rhetorical process in operation here which strongly implies that the statement under consideration is context-free while at the same time a very carefully prepared context within the text is being developed.

Basic Design and the Metaphor of Physics

The second influence on basic design teaching was relativity theory.

Not surprisingly the most influential and prestigious theory of physics in this century had an enormous impact in other areas. Relativity theory owed its success partly to the conceptualisation of space and time as a dynamic system of interacting forces. This was picked up by Gestalt theorists as a potential model of the neurological processes that guided perceptual experience. This model has since been rejected by neurologists but the extension of the metaphor into the conceptualisation of pictorial space persists in Basic Design.

The idea that the picture space on a page in a book can be seen as a dynamic field is one of the most important contributions of the Basic Design Course to the style of twentieth-century visual communication. The proponents of Basic Design developed a vocabulary of pictorial space based on the vocabulary of physics and biology.

Every living organism — be it a plant, an animal, a human being or a social structure — is a relatively constant form . . . To maintain the same constant structure every living organism must achieve a dynamic unity. The plastic image (picture) is no exception. Only by dynamic order can it become a living form of human experience. (Kepes, 1944, p. 30)

It is important to bear in mind that this is a metaphor. It is an extremely powerful one and has provided a seemingly endless array of visual possibilities. It is also important to realise that the distinction between metaphor and actuality is constantly blurred by the teachers of Basic Design.

Horizontals and verticals operating together introduce the principle of balanced oppositions of tensions. The vertical expresses a force which is of primary significance — gravitational pull, the horizontal again contributes a primary sensation — a supporting flatness; the two together produce a deeply satisfying resolved feeling, perhaps because together they symbolise the human experience of absolute balance, of standing erect on level ground. (Sausmarez, 1964, p. 21)

Basic Design teachers believe that they are working with the fundamental stuff of visual experience: that they have discovered the 'language of vision'. The consequence of this is an intense preoccupation with the 'internal dynamics' of the picture or the page. Not only the content of the page or picture receives attention but the 'empty' space is carefully scrutinised and 'balanced'. It is these conceptions which

Figure 12

THE WORKS

OF

THE BRITISH DRAMATISTS.

𝕮arefully 𝕾electeð from tðe 𝕭est 𝕰ðitions,

WITH

COPIOUS NOTES, BIOGRAPHIES, AND A HISTORICAL INTRODUCTION.

BY JOHN S. KELTIE, F.S.A. SCOT.,

ELITOR OF ' DEFOE'S WORKS,' ETC.

WILLIAM P. NIMMO & CO.,
EDINBURGH.
1879.

Figure 13

A basic course in

GRAPHIC DESIGN

Richard Taylor

Studio Vista: London
Van Nostrand Reinhold Company:
New York

Source: with permission of Studio Vista, London.

mark the difference between the design in Figure 12 which is a typical example of nineteenth-century typographic conventions and Figure 13 which is a 'sensitively' designed page of this century.

The question students like to ask of this self-conscious design is whether it makes any difference to the reader. As we shall see there is some evidence, not surprisingly, that the spatial arrangement of information on a page can influence its comprehension but this in many respects is too simple a way of framing both the question and the answer.

It should be clear that an understanding of the difference between Figures 12 and 13 is crucially dependent on one's understanding of the conception of space developed by teachers of Basic Design. Since it is based on a very elaborate metaphor one needs to be privy to that metaphor and have some practice in its application before one can appreciate its design qualities. However the teachers of Basic Design argue that they are tapping a deep and universal process of visual information-processing; therefore one does not need to understand consciously what has been done, one simply has to look and the design by its very structure will guide the eye to an economical comprehension of its meaning. The process is unconscious. Bearing in mind that this claim is based on an inadequate theory of human information-processing and that no substantive corroborative evidence for the claim exists other than the objectified experience of designers, it must be treated with scepticism.

It would be wrong to dismiss, on the basis of this scepticism, the contribution of Basic Design to visual communication practice in this century. First, it has fostered a kind of enquiry, albeit formal and phenomenological, into the processes of visual perception. This has considerably enlarged the range of graphic alternatives available to designers and we must take very seriously the opinions of those who have spent a lifetime choosing and manipulating images even if this has been done in a relatively isolated context. Secondly, it does not follow logically that because a theory is incorrect the practice associated with it is necessarily so; but we must rightly view with scepticism any assertion about the practice which has been based on an appeal to the theory. Thirdly, while the specific articulations of pictorial space by teachers of Basic Design may be idiosyncratic, there can be little doubt that they are generally correct in stressing that perception is organised. Perhaps it is that single fact coupled with our constant objectification of meaning that provides the backbone of any visual communication. Finally, their use of physical and biological metaphors has provided an intriguing and seemingly endless source of delight in pattern-making which might be better understood if the formal constraints under which it is executed are more fully understood.

Education and Communication Effectiveness

In this chapter I have examined the author/message relation, in particular the professional communicator, and I have singled out the Bauhaus as one of the most important influences on current practice. The critical lesson is that professional practice *per se* is no guarantee of effectiveness. Employing highly trained designers to produce educational material cannot resolve the issue of effectiveness because of the tendency of current practitioners to look inwards. The institutional framework in which communication occurs, the professional values of practitioners, and the traditions of skill, all conspire, perhaps unintentionally, to set apart the author/message relation from the audience/message relation. From what has been said it is possible to isolate and identify two sources of errors of judgement on the part of the author, namely the inferred audience and objectification. If the presumptions about the audience are at odds with the actual audience there is almost certain to be a loss of effectiveness. Objectification presents very special problems which will be dealt with when we come to consider the kinds of strategies necessary to change current practice. This chapter has in a very general way identified some of the issues, and highlights the lack of any real direct control that the author might have on the audience/message relation. Whether learning takes place or not would seem to be more related to the flexibility, ingenuity, motivation and patience of the learner rather than to the sensitivity and skill of the communicator, and it is towards an exploration of these that we will turn in the next chapter.

4 VISUAL COMMUNICATION AND THE STUDENT

Introduction

Long before children confront their first slide and tape programme, illustrated text or schools broadcast, they have encountered the television set, picture books and the back of the cereal pack. The means of communication which educators have been so eager to embrace are widely exploited in mass communication, and our initial and basic familiarity with these forms comes not from the classroom but from the ubiquitous mass media. In so far as it is appropriate to say that we learn how to 'read' pictures, television or the cinema, our first and often only lessons come from repeated exposure to the popular use of these forms, which are now part of the fabric of our culture.

The educational use of visual communication (with the exception of literacy, numeracy and certain specialised skills like mapping or technical drawing), depends heavily on the assumptions that the skills of 'reading' have been acquired elsewhere, or that no skills are necessary at all. Literacy and numeracy skills are continuously monitored as students progress from infant school up to tertiary education. Every effort is expended to ensure basic mastery in these vital social skills. But, even if one takes account of the current vogue in media studies and the confused area of art education, there is no equivalent pressure to acquire skills in the 'reading' of drawings, photographs, television or cinema. The audience/message relation in most forms of educational visual communication is an unanalysed given. Despite the increasing use of a widening variety of forms of visual communication within the education system our knowledge of how students learn from these media is lamentably poor. Part of the reason for this ignorance, as Schramm has suggested, is due to asking the wrong sorts of questions (Chapter 2), but behind that lies a conceptual malaise; in this chapter I will try to remedy this by clarifying the way we formulate our questions.

In general terms I will be concerned with how we can organise our thinking about the audience/message relation, using pictures, the basis of many uses of visual communication, to exemplify the kinds of issues and problems that can arise. Much of what follows is a tentative exploration drawing on ideas from semiotics which are seldom aired within the education literature. Even the term 'semiotics' may be unfamiliar to many educationalists, so it is necessary first to explain its scope and significance.

What is 'Semiotics'?

It would be misleading at this stage in its history to describe semiotics as a discipline of a subject. It would be more appropriate to think of it either as an emerging discipline or as a programme for generating one (Eco, 1977). Semiotics is an attempt to bring together under a common framework all the diverse forms of communication which are to be found both in human and in animal life — it could include, for example, bird calls, bee dancing, television programmes, writing, speaking, sign language and even the transmission of genetic information by DNA. Some see its scope as even wider, embracing virtually anything that could be described as having an organised system of meanings for its users; this would include such things as fashion, table manners and architecture (Barthes, 1967; Lévi-Strauss, 1979; Eco, 1972). Such an ambitious venture is essentially a product of twentieth-century thought though its roots go back much further. It has been characterised to date, particularly among European scholars, by a heavy dependence on linguistics as a model for enquiry into other meaning systems (Barthes, 1967). This is unfortunate for a variety of reasons (see below). It has also, regrettably, been characterised by a great deal of loose thinking, rampant verbosity and unsubstantiated claims which have made much of it both inaccessible and unattractive to all but the most devoted students. This has in many ways obscured what is a very important attempt to provide a sensible framework for understanding our communication experience, by bringing together all the divergent disciplines which have separately examined only aspects of it (Eco, 1977; Sebeok, 1976). In what follows I shall be drawing more on the spirit than the substance of the venture but it should be clear that the implications for education of such a venture are far reaching.

If we are ever able to relate media to learning effectiveness for a particular task in any except the most general way (picture? print?) it will probably come about through understanding the unique strengths and capabilities of the different symbolic coding systems. That is the window we presently stand looking through. (Schramm, 1977, p. 274)

It is the rugged and unformed landscape of semiotics that beckons through that window.

The Atypical Nature of Language

Now that the origins of the analysis which is to follow are clear, I want to be contrary, and dissociate myself from one of its main props: namely the use of language as a paradigm for all other forms of communication. This use takes three forms: the explicit use of language as a model (Barthes, 1967); the implicit use of language and language metaphors to describe non-linguistic communication (e.g. Kepes, 1944; Metz, 1974; Coward and Ellis, 1977; Fiske and Hartley, 1978; Williamson, 1978); and the use of the methods of linguistics for investigating non-linguistic communication.

Such terms as 'language of vision', 'language of the self', 'film language', 'the codes of television', 'decoding advertisements', all give an impression of sharing with language an underlying similarity which makes it possible to analyse concepts in a quasi-linguistic manner. To suggest that there are similarities of this kind is very tempting because it opens up a rich vein of gems and possible nuggets of insight. Unfortunately it is fool's gold; language is unique. There is a stark biological and cultural contrast between language and other forms of communication. With the exception of gesture, language is the only system of communication for which we are naturally equipped — the ability to speak, at least potentially, is a biological given. This in itself is a sufficent basis for describing language as atypical. Again with the exception of gesture, it is a communication skill which is developed very early. It is encouraged almost universally and seldom is there a shortage of models to copy. It is generally regarded as the primary means of communication. The skills associated with language are systematically extended and developed in our society through the school system's commitment to mass literacy. This has tended to homogenise its use within any particular language culture, with some standardisation of pronunciation, vocabulary, spelling and grammar.

No other system of communication can claim the prodigious application of scholarship that language enjoys; dictionaries, thesauruses, guides to grammar and seemingly endless studies of language and literature all contribute to an identifiable language culture which is highly articulate, self-conscious and above all shared more widely than any other system of communication. It is this that enabled the French linguist Ferdinand de Saussure, who had a seminal influence on the development of semiotics, to assert with confidence:

> Language exists in the form of a sum of impressions deposited in the brain of each member of a community, almost like a dictionary of which identical copies have been distributed to each individual. Language exists in each individual, yet is common to all. (Saussure, 1974, p. 19)

Saussure is careful to point out that there is variability:

> Among all the individuals that are linked together by speech some sort of average will be set up: all will reproduce — not exactly of course, but approximately — the same signs united with the same concepts. (ibid., p. 13)

Thus the impression is generated of a shared code which can be analysed quite separately from its individual users. But even with the massive cultural emphasis on language there is, as Saussure and other linguists acknowledge, variability in usage. It is this variability that provoked Saussure to make the important distinction between the system of language (*la langue*) and the individual speech act (*parole*) and which gave rise to the distinction between competence and performance in the theories of the celebrated American linguist Noam Chomsky (see also Chapter 2, p.34). Even if there is some basis for an idealised notion of language as a structural system based on the unique position which language enjoys, there are two important reasons why such an approach to other forms of communication, particularly in education, must be viewed with suspicion.

First, there is no *logical* reason to suppose that non-linguistic communication such as film, television, painting or photography enjoys a widely shared and uniformly applied code. It is not a necessary consequence of their existence. As was clear from Chapter 3, the self-sustaining environment of the professionals demands only the *presumption* that such a code exists. Since these forms are widely available and used it would be improbable to suggest that there was no shared basis for their understanding, but exactly what that basis might be and whether it exists in the same form uniformly throughout our society is a matter for empirical enquiry, not *a priori* presumption. The trap into which many semioticians have fallen is to presume that because a code can be constructed by a close study of the message, that code is necessarily commonly used.

As I have previously shown, the only logical necessity, a consequence of according communication status to anything, and a function of the schema used, is to *construct* the meaning within the framework provided by the *inferred* author and the physical form of the message. There is no absolute requirement that meaning must be determined by appeal to a shared code. For example, empirical investigation shows repeatedly that even in an area of social priority like the highway code, where there is a strong pragmatic imperative, the degree of comprehension of the 'dictionary definition' of pictorial symbols is alarmingly low.

The second reason for doubting the value of a quasi-linguistic approach to other forms of communication is because variability in student performance is at the very core of the problems associated with using the media for learning. Any theoretical stance which idealises the process of communication at the expense of individual differences will simply end up being both normative and prescriptive. Instead of suggesting what range of variability might be expected and hence what control might be exercised in the learning enviroment to aid the student, educational technologists confront us simply with a description of message content and how students ought to respond to it.

One final retreat is left for the linguaphile and that is to suggest that there are deep structures which are shared by all. This is the assertion of contemporary linguistics in the Chomskian tradition; and as we saw in Chapter 3, Gestalt theory, which claimed to discover universal laws of visual organisation, has been used as one of the main theoretical supports for visual communication practice. It is also currently claimed by some psychologists that our ability to read pictures is unlearnt. With these claims in mind we can begin an examination of pictorial communication and consider the importance of these claims for education.

Is the Perception of Pictures Learnt?

The evidence in relation to this question has been previously reviewed (Kennedy, 1974) but using the same information I find myself drawn to a very different conclusion. Kennedy regards an experiment conducted by Hochberg and Brooks (Hochberg and Brooks, 1962) as crucial evidence in favour of the view that the perception of pictures is unlearnt. By any standards it is a poor experiment. Hochberg and his wife tried to bring up their child in an environment free of pictorial material and then to determine whether the child could identify everyday objects from their representation in pictures. From birth, the boy had been taught names of toys and other solid objects, whose colours, with two exceptions, were either uniform or divided into functional areas. He was never told or allowed to overhear the name or meaning of any picture of depicted object. 'In fact, pictures were, in general, kept from his immediate vicinity' (p. 625). But, continued the authors, 'this is not to say that [he] never had been exposed to pictures' (p. 625). A print on the wall, 'a myriad of billboards' along the highways; accidental encounters of picture books and glimpses of food labels (books and food-cans gently removed, with no instruction or naming-play); and the two exceptions mentioned above — a top with pictures of elves, and a high-chair with a decal of babies, accordingly available only under strict supervision to prevent naming in his presence. Constant vigilance was the watchword for this experiment.

> By 19 months of age, the child began actively to seek pictures. . . [he] became aware of events on the TV set in the next room, managed to obtain a glimpse of the screen on which a horse was being depicted, and excitedly cried 'dog'; . . . about the same time, pointing to the decal [on the high chair] said 'baby'. (p. 626)

Parental response was soon unavoidable, and testing began at that point.

The testing revealed that the child had no difficulty in naming familiar objects from line drawings and photographs, and they concluded:

> the complete absence of instruction in the present case (the absence of 'association' between picture and represented object) points to some irreducible minimum of native ability for pictorial recognition. (ibid., p. 628)

There are a number of problems with this experiment that do not warrant the above conclusion. First, generalisations based on one case, however spectacular, are of dubious value. Secondly, it is clear from the above account that the environment was not susceptible to even partial control. If this seems to reflect on the experimenters' lack of diligence it would be very salutary to try just for one day to count the number of unavoidable encounters one has with pictorial material in an urban environment. Thirdly, it is presumed that learning can only take place where there is instruction; but there is ample evidence from the casual observation of many living organisms, let alone those as sophisticated as children, that learning can and does take place because of the motivations and curiosity of the organism, without intervention by an external 'instructor'. Finally, unless there is some ambiguity which has escaped this reader's attention, it clearly says in their account that the child began actively to seek pictures before the commencement of testing. This would suggest that the child had the concept 'picture' which, whether acquired before or after identifying its first object in a picture, certainly invalidates the testing and consequent results as evidence for unlearnt picture perception — unless the experimenters wanted to argue that the *concept* of picture was innate!

This leads me to reject the tests and conclusions. I remain interested, nevertheless, in explaining the child's behaviour up to the commencement of testing, and tentatively offer an alternative hypothesis; that learning to identify objects from pictures involves the learning of a principle — a rule. The rule put very simply would be that anything which is distinguishable from an object can be used to stand for that object. This, superficially, seems to be suggesting the opposite to what a picture seems to do — it seems to stand for an object by being in some manner equivalent to it.

Just before the age of two most children are going through a very active period of language acquisition. The principle which I have just mentioned is implicit in naming. Words are distinguishable from the objects they represent and from each other. Suppose that the child, instead of learning each individual name with its object, as a separate task, learns the principle, i.e. sounds can stand for objects. Once so equipped, learning the words for objects can proceed very rapidly. The limits are set then by the child's environment and the fineness of discrimination that the child can make in hearing and speech. But it is not only sounds which are used in this way. Gesture can 'stand for', and so can toys; in fact the world is full of 'stand-for' possibilities. Recall your own excitement at discovering a new principle or truth; there is a strong urge to try it out whenever possible. I suspect that, full of this excitement, the uninstructed child confronts its first picture with the question 'what can this stand for?' In identifying that it is somehow different from other objects the child might also be struck by its resemblance to known objects and suddenly a new 'stand-for' relation is discovered — not based on difference but on similarity. The similarity may be of feature, or optic array, or a mixture of both, with arbitrary components as well. Either or all can lead to this new kind of standing-for relation. No wonder the Hochberg's child started looking for pictures! And as with other 'stand-for' relations, the child seeks an active response from others. This is a very simplified account of an extremely intricate process. The acquisition of language involves far more than just the rules for naming, and the recognition of objects in pictures must, because of the variety of different kinds of pictures, be explained in more than one way. What I think is simple is the basic principle behind picture perception, the 'stand-for' rule, which has already been learnt in relation to other material and is simply extended to another feature of the child's environment.

This account is consistent with other data in the field. O'Connor and Hermelin (1961) showed that children with a mean IQ of 50 could identify objects named from pictures of these objects. This suggests that pictures are at least no more difficult than the spoken word when it comes to 'stand-for' relations. The absence of a 'stand-for' rule in infants accounts for the results in the work of Bower (1964) in which he trained infants a few months old to respond to a solid cube, but despite transfer of training to other cubes, he could elicit no significant response to a picture of the cube. Bower argues that the absence of kinetic and binocular information in the picture must account for the lack of response. Clearly then the child can discriminate between the real cube and the picture of the cube. What is missing though is the rule which would enable the infant to make the connections between object and picture. In a later experiment (1971) Bower provided infants with stereoscopic pictures and in that situation they took the depicted objects to be real — but this has nothing to do with the perception of pictures. It merely demonstrates the limited perceptual judgement of an infant under highly contrived circumstances. The fact that the infants tried to reach for the objects depicted and were distressed when they couldn't, demonstrates that they didn't like the trick. Children, even when encountering their first pictures do not, to the best of my knowledge, react in this fashion to what is depicted in pictures. There is a clear understanding of the 'stand-for' relation. It is quite clear that in Bower's earlier experiment the infant could discriminate between an object and a picture of that object but had no conception of the 'stand-for' rule. In the later experiment discrimination was simply confounded.

Evidence is often offered in support of the claim that perception of pictures is unlearnt from *trompe l'oeil*, that is, situations where painted or depicted objects are mistakenly taken for real objects. However, all that this evidence actually shows is that people can make mistakes when presented with carefully contrived situations, which is not very surprising and merely confuses the issue. Equally, evidence from animal studies which show animals reacting without prior training to pictures of objects as if they were actual objects also confuses the issue since the question of pictorial perception is being conflated with the problem of mistaken perception, and these are of course quite different. Finally the cross-cultural evidence is in the main too ambiguous to help resolve the issue. I have to suggest then, that contrary to Kennedy's assessment, the perception of pictures is in an important sense learnt. This learning consists of acquiring the concept of pictures which enables an application of the 'stand-for' rule. It is obvious from studies of children and from cross-cultural studies that this initial, gross, application of the rule presents few problems. It is clear however that some difficulties are present because in very few cases do experimenters report 100 per cent correct identification of objects from their depiction. If the author/message relation is studied, it is possible to describe the logical connection between a picture and what it represents; but the audience is not necessarily privy to this logical relation, only to the picture. The errors made may well be due to the audience searching the picture using an inappropriate kind of logical relation, but the mistake made by a great many researchers in this field is to presume that it is the picture itself which determines the response. As a consequence there has been a sterile debate about whether pictures work by somehow being like the objects they depict, or whether they work by a system of conventions like language where the relation between the objects and the symbolic devices used to depict them is arbitrary. If we accept as a presupposition the prior acquisition of the concept 'picture' which precipitates the 'stand-for' rule, then the problem disappears, because the 'stand-for' rule initiates a search for pictorial meaning. In a very important logical sense one recognises a picture before one knows what it is a picture of or how it pictures. Almost every picture which is used in a picturing way exists in a context — in a book, on a poster, in a frame, etc., which tells the user that he is looking at a picture. (Many people become very upset when they see modern non-figurative art because no matter what kind of stand-for rules of depiction they apply, the picture does not yield to a figurative meaning and they feel they are somehow being cheated.) The depiction of the human form on the Arecibo message is in some respects quite arbitrary by comparison with the equivalent depictions on the Pioneer plaque. It is also interesting to compare depiction of the solar system on the Pioneer plaque with its counterpart on the Arecibo message. There is in the Arecibo message a crude convention which is arbitrary with respect to all features except planetary position and size, and even the latter convention is inconsistently used as the four inner planets are assumed to be of the same size! None the less, there is an important sense in which we would describe them all as pictures, but this has only a little to do with their intrinsic properties and a great deal to do with the stand-for rule we apply to them.

Note how crude this rule is and how much inconsistency it can tolerate. As we can see it is extraordinarily flexible but its applications are riddled with ambiguities and inconsistencies. For example, the Arecibo message makes use of a number of arbitrary codes where what is represented can in no sense be said to look like the symbols used. There are some non-arbitrary codes like those used to show the shapes of the telescope, the human and DNA, which in a sense look like the thing represented except that the telescope is represented in cross section. Each of these relies on various additional codes which do not have the same logical relation to what they represent. However, it is one thing for me to notice and point out these ambiguities with my knowledge of the author/message relation and a background in logical and scientific analysis, but it is quite another to suggest that these subtleties enter into the crude application of the 'stand-for' rule by a lay audience. They are simply not noticed because the schema available does not contain any knowledge of them and therefore does not attempt to construct them from the available information.

This brings us back to the theory of perception that was developed briefly in Chapter 1. Perception is active; we search our environment, we interrogate it, and we look and ask questions in terms of the concepts available to us. If our conception of pictures is crude, then our perception of pictures will be crude. Psychologists have wasted a great deal of effort trying to find out whether people can make judgements of depth from pictures, but how many of us actually use pictures in that way? Even when we look at a perfect rendering in perspective, how important is it whether something is thirty yards or forty yards away from the observer, so long as it is roughly convincing? If for some reason it became necessary to make these kind of judgements then the skill could be acquired and no doubt more of us would become conscious of the many ambiguities and inconsistencies which for a variety of reasons occur throughout the history of perspective; but to the uneducated eye they are simply not there. Psychologists would be far better investigating how one might develop this skill of making depth judgements from pictures, rather than asking people who only vaguely use depth to make vague judgements and arguing that their findings are contributing to our knowledge of pictorial perception. It is rather like pointing out that someone used to wielding a stone axe is clumsy with a scalpel. In educational terms it comes down to making sure the student is aware of the potential of what is offered.

The Picture in our Culture

This brings us to a consideration of what kind of expectations students may have of pictorial material. I began this chapter by saying that our pictorial education, such as it is, takes place outside the classroom in the world of popular culture. This sets up certain kinds of expectations which are in many respects narrow and misleading. It is always important to distinguish between the logical possibilities for using pictures and the everyday uses that people actually make of them. Most people do not think very deeply about pictures. There is very little that they encounter which might provoke thought and even less opportunity to nourish and sustain such thoughts as do arise. Simply, pictures are not normally the sort of objects on which we care to exercise our intelligence.

Generalisations about popular conceptions in any area are problematic particularly when these are based on impressions rather than carefully sifted evidence. What follows then is a sketch. It is offered here as an indication of the kind of factors that can contribute towards basic expectations of students to pictorial material. There are many individual differences and as our society changes so the way we use different artefacts changes. Those used for communication play a particularly important role because they in turn shape the nature of individuality. Any educator must draw his or her own sketch of student expectations which will differ from one culture to another and will vary across individuals. But the basic questions will remain the same: What are the main contexts in which pictures are used, and for what kinds of purposes? What sources of information are commonly available to students about pictorial material?

My sketch begins with incidents from childhood. Children's books are full of pictures. There is therefore an early link established between pictures and narrative. A close examination of most children's books will reveal that the pictures play a supportive, confirmatory and often purely decorative role. There are exceptions: for example, Graham Oakley's stories of the church cat and mice (Oakley, 1972), where the narrative is a combination of words and pictures and a great deal is missed if the pictures are not examined carefully. The most obvious exception is the comic. But something happens to the relative emphasis given to words and pictures as the child grows. The changes probably begin with the beginning of schooling. The child coming home from school with a picture in one hand and a piece of writing in the other, soon discovers that parents are not only interested in the writing but have a much wider range of critical comments to make about it. Its neatness, accuracy, spelling, grammar and meaning can all be criticised. By contrast the picture presents most parents with some difficulty. 'How nice, what pretty colours, what is it?' probably covers the full range of their critical vocabulary. If it is liked, it might be stuck on to the fridge door. (This puts it in a particular context about which more later.) Teachers and parents follow the development of children's literary skills. Reading is maintained and slowly the difficulty of material is increased. All this takes place initially in books which contain illustrations but no careful attention is devoted to the 'reading' of the pictures. So a contrast is established between the importance of written material and the relative unimportance of pictorial material. This reinforces the proposition that pictures are very simple and self-evident, and no special training in their reading is required.

The notion that pictures are simple derives sustenance from other sources. The explanation of perception offered in Chapter 1 is radically at odds with common-sense notions where seeing and thinking are quite separate. Hence the contrast between words and pictures manifests itself in a slightly different way. Words are associated with thinking but pictures are associated with seeing; one is an intellectual activity, the other purely sensory and therefore simply a matter of picking up the information which is there. The development of photography has done much to disguise the real potential complexity of pictures; the manufacturers of cheap cameras, ever since the first box Brownie, have followed the slogan 'You simply press the button', so the activity is not only simple, it is actually mindless. An examination of advertisements for cheap cameras reveals a displacement of the problems associated with taking photographs from the perceptual to the technical realm. This is an obvious by-product of the fact that the manufacturer is more interested in selling cameras than giving the population an education in picture-taking. It is very likely that the public's continuing dissatisfaction with its picture-taking skills is a persistent source of motivation for buying yet another new camera with the latest technical innovation that makes it all even simpler. There is nothing that provides any information on the real cognitive problems associated with photography, and hence there is nothing within what is probably the commonest form of picture-making in our society, to question the presumption that pictures are simple.

However, there is a yet cruder conception of pictures which strips them even of their communicative function and reduces them to information. There is a certain sense in which photographs and, to some extent, other pictures, particularly perspective pictures are, because of their apparent closeness to nature, treated as if they were windows on to the world. This is not surprising, indeed the origins of optical perspective and realism can be traced to the use of real windows by artists to construct pictorial space.

The idea of pictures as windows carries over into film and televison where it has a voyeuristic quality. It is as if one were looking in unbeknown to the actors, watching their actions, from an unobserved point 'somewhere out there'. This provides an illusion of neutrality and objectivity but in order to question the illusion the inferred author is suppressed, thus blurring the distinction between communication and information (see Chapter 6). One can see how this blurring affects the way in which pictures are defined. Kennedy for example says picturing '. . . is purely a means of *communicating*, showing, beholding. Picturing, at heart, is a means for *informing* people about visible things . . . ' (p. 4) (my italics). Notice how it is the picture which in Kennedy's account is the active agent, the independent entity. It follows from this that a good picture is one which shows clearly what it is a picture of. The window must be nice and clear!

There is another popular conception of pictures which draws not on the suppression of authorship but on the definite attribution of authorship to a particular kind of person — the artist. Once again we can return to our eager young pupil, browbeaten over poor spelling and grammar but whose picture has been stuck with sticky tape and approval on to the fridge door. It is a curious phenomenon of our society that the most unaccomplished scribble made by children is hailed as 'art'. No one would regard those first attempts at writing as literature or poetry but it seems that the untutored attempts at picture-making can bypass all the usual criteria of craftsmanship and excellence and emerge fully formed to be displayed where nobody could miss them.

It is accepted without question by many that there is nothing strange in calling the graphic output of children, 'art'. But it is a fact which can be ascertained by going to any magazine stand that the world is full of pictures which in the main have many other uses apart from 'art'; very few indeed are likely candidates for such a designation. So why are these childhood drawings seen only in such a narrow context? To understand this it is necessary to realise that the romantic tradition going back to Rousseau's idea of the noble savage has permeated our popular conception of both art and artists. Art of any kind, romanticism has it, is the product of the inner self which is unfettered by social constraints. The uninstructed mark-making of children is believed to be a kind of embryonic art flowing straight from that inner self without the mediation of social conventions and skills, and is hence 'pure' self-expression.

This has led to a misguided, but unfortunately very influential theory of art education which has earned the dubious distinction of claiming that any kind of teaching in art can damage the mind (Read, 1958; Lowenfeld and Brittain, 1970). The consequence of this view in educational terms has been that in many schools the only area where children could have had an opportunity to develop an awareness of the complexities of pictures and picture-making has been the art room and art class; and here the teacher has been reluctant to do so for fear of harming them. So while the rest of the school is busily buying up all manner of audio-visual aids, the art room is turning its back on the cumulative skills that make such visual delights possible. The association between picture-making and art is maintained and with it the popular conception of the artist which is of someone inclined to be mad, to live in a garret, die without recognition and leave a legacy of illegitimate children. This is of course a travesty but it is hardly likely to persuade parents to encourage children to become artists, which is yet another reason why pictures and picturing skills have a low social priority. There is the more flattering romantic view of the artist as a radical free-thinker who stands above other mortals and whose works revolutionise our view of the world. In either case the roots of his power are personal, unlearnt and mysterious — a gift of the gods. This has been institutionalised in our art galleries which significantly at times seem to imitate Greek temples with the paintings as oracles, their meanings elusively out of reach of ordinary mortals and only mediated through an elite priesthood of curators and art experts. The lay person can only stand in awe.

Thus my sketch of the expectations students may have of pictorial material reveals two polarities: simplification and mystification. Pictures are either unworthy of our intelligence or beyond it. Whether this sketch is correct is a matter for empirical enquiry of a kind not normally engaged in at present. I hope it helps to emphasise the point that knowledge about student expectations is an essential part of our understanding of the audience/message relation as it arrives untutored into the classroom, lecture theatre or seminar room.

We do not as a matter of course provide people with an education in how to use pictures in order to learn. To invoke the contrast with language yet again, skills in comprehension, precis, style, argument and reasoning all form part of language education in schools to enable students to use language as an aid to learning. There is no equivalent for picturing. If we are satisfied with the kinds of skills and expectations students bring to pictorial material we need go no further, but if we wish to extend and develop the use of pictorial material in education we must not only expose students to more of it, we must also change their expectations so that they are prepared to take the best advantage of what is offered. Thus the further use of visual material in education must go hand in hand with firstly an understanding of the audience/message relation and secondly a changing if necessary of that relation. We cannot use film, television or drawings as aids to learning unless we also show *how* people can learn from these forms.

The Empirical Study of the Audience/Message Relation

With a few exceptions most of the research conducted in the relation between pictures and learning ignores the above and presumes that skills in using pictorial material are fully developed and that the task of research is essentially descriptive and comparative (Fleming, 1979); that is, to map out what those skills are and to compare them with other symbolic processes. However, as Fleming points out:

> Probably the picture effect of most far reaching significance to date is the effect on the infomation processing skills and strategies of the

viewer. One way this idea is currently conceptualised is as 'visual literacy'. Through much exposure to pictures, people not only become 'literate' in reading pictures but in the process their ways of thinking may be modified. (Fleming, 1979, pp. 242-3)

Certainly the wide availability of pictorial material is an important factor but that in itself is not enough. If, as is often claimed by media critics, more has only meant more of the same, then the sheer mass of material will stifle the range of skills that develop, not elaborate them. A wide variety of pictorial material, however diverse and exotic, will if labelled 'ephemeral' and 'trivial', be carefully screened out of the serious business of learning, whatever it may do to our cognitive processes. Such has, until recently, been the fate of the comic strip. The discovery that the imaginative and narrative possibilities of comic strips were being exploited by children in their spontaneous drawing activity (Wilson and Wilson, 1977) is an indication of the changing attitudes towards the role such culturally available forms can play in the personal cognitive development of children. The full range of possibilities from this remains to be explored (Duncum, 1980). However, it is clear that art educators are divided on whether respectable status should be accorded to this 'copying' (Arnheim, 1978), thus reflecting the inbuilt prejudices against certain symbolic forms. No proper account of the media in education can be given without taking these prejudices into account. However, they are not timeless, they shift and change in many subtle ways, making it necessary constantly to redefine the preferred forms of communication.

The search for invariants — generalisations that will be useful over a long period of time — has not been fruitful. The empirical research has in this respect been very disappointing. It is argued by those who wish to pursue their research in the hypothetico-deductive tradition that in the past the area has suffered either from lack of empirical rigour or (more convincingly) because of poor conceptualisation. While both of these may be true of the past, it is still the case that present research, with all its refinements, does not bring us closer to a refinement of educational practice because there is no effective way to translate the results of such study into a framework for educational practice.

5   LEARNING AND THE FORCES OF CHANGE

Introduction

I come now to the confluence of ideas which have been developed in the preceding chapters. Visual communication is a process with two foci, the author/message and the audience/message; each functions within a framework of assumptions and expectations. There is, as I have shown, no necessary logical basis for presuming that there is a nexus between them. They represent two worlds in which the only unconditional similarities are the physical form of the message and the humanity of the participants. Yet what lies at the heart of any communication process is at least the hope that these two worlds may somehow come together. In education that hope focuses on learning.

Learning, however that process is conceived, provides the ultimate rationale for the use of visual communication in education. It is because of the belief that textbooks, television and many other forms of media have some distinctive role in learning that educators use them among the tools of their craft.

There are a variety of questions, empirical, conceptual and cultural, that can be asked about learning. The nature of the psychological and neurological basis of learning has been an empirical question which has preoccupied many psychologists, although much of the discussion has taken place within the impoverished conceptual framework of behaviourism, which has meant that only a very limited notion of learning, that of stimulus–response contingencies, has been thoroughly investigated. It is now recognised that a full account of learning must incorporate many more varieties of learning than classical or operant conditioning. What is not always recognised is that the enlarged view of learning is not due to new empirical findings so much as to a new conceptualisation of the learning process. The empirical evidence has followed on from this. Stepping back from the immediate interplay of conceptions formulated into testable hypotheses it is possible to show that different concepts of learning spring from different epistemological frameworks — beneath ideas about learning are assumptions about the nature of knowledge. The varieties of learning can be seen to be drawing on a range of philosophical interpretations. Taking yet another step back one may wonder why

79

certain conceptions are considered worthy of attention at any particular time, and here it is possible to point to the cultural milieu in which the investigator finds himself. Nowhere is this clearer than in the recent elaborations of the concepts of learning which have responded to the huge growth of educational technology.

However, the expansion has been largely in the area of hardware and personnel. The theory underlying the practice is still in a process of development and, while there are some very interesting ideas currently being investigated, it would be true to say that we do not have at the moment a satisfactory theory of learning in relation to the media; moreover (as will already be clear from previous chapters), we still need a way to link adequately such theory to pedagogic practice. In this chapter I shall examine the practical consequences of some of the theories in this area. I will be less concerned with their empirical validity than with their capacity to translate into decision-making, and the extent to which they are likely to develop a sensitivity to the educational potential of media.

Learning — the Systems Approach

Among educational technologists the systems approach has been extremely popular. Basically it consists of defining the educational process as means/end activity. One begins by specifying the desired outcome, then decides how to achieve this outcome, and finally, one conducts some evaluation to determine whether the desired outcome has resulted. It seems extremely logical and moreover implies that the educator has a high degree of control over the learning environment. It is asserted, often as a matter of faith by the advocates of this approach, that 'systematically designed instruction can greatly affect individual human development' and also that

> Unplanned and undirected learning, we believe, is almost certain to lead to the development of individuals who are in one way or another incompetent to derive personal satisfaction from living in our society of today and tomorrow. A fundamental reason for instructional design is to ensure that no one is 'educationally disadvantaged', that everyone has an equal opportunity to use his (or her) individual talents to the fullest degree. (Gagné and Briggs, 1974, p. 5)

There is no doubt that two kinds of learning are being suggested here — planned and directed versus unplanned and undirected. It is also clear which of these is regarded as acceptable. Moreover, everyone will have an opportunity to develop their talents (except presumably those with a talent for unplanned and undirected learning!). The reader may or may not agree with the basic conservatism of the underlying ideology or with its simplistic statement of liberal values, but apart from that there are certain logical entailments that need to be developed.

Turning to the unacceptable face of learning, the unplanned and undirected — does it simply disappear? It is not mentioned again in the above text and we might be forgiven if we presumed that it simply does not occur. This suggests an extraordinary degree of control of the learning environment by the instructor and that in itself might seem a very seductive proposition. There can be no mistaking the confidence with which it is offered.

> The task of instructional planning can be vastly simplified by assigning objectives to five major categories of human capabilities. Such categories can be formed because each leads to a different class of human performance, and each requires a different set of instructional conditions for effective learning. Within each category, regardless of the subject matter of instruction, the same conditions apply. (ibid., p. 23)

It sounds extremely convincing; the jargon of educational objectives, human capabilities, performance and evaluation has turned the head of many an audio-visual lover. But it is not a recipe for educational bliss. The power of the instructor is largely illusory, because, as will become apparent, there is no adequate theoretical basis for linking objectives with media and therefore with learning. Media selection is not even an inexact science. Despite the impressive vocabulary, when science fails, the instructor has to rely on that good old standby — human judgement.

If one were to accept the extreme empiricism on which some of the notions of the systems approach are founded, it would still be the case that the environment of each learner would present many subtly different stimuli that would be beyond the control of the instructor even during the instructional event. In the controlled environment of the Skinner box (the paradigm for this kind of learning) psychologists have to go to extraordinary lengths to prevent even the wretched rat from attending to the 'wrong' stimulus. The instructional environment is, thankfully, much richer in information.

However, the main crisis of control comes from the problems within the system of relating media to outcomes.

> Materials for instruction need to reflect not simply what their author knows, but also how the student is intended to learn such knowledge. Accordingly, instructional design must take fully into account *learning conditions* that need to be established in order for the desired effects to occur. (ibid., p. 6)

Thus control depends not only on an all-powerful instructor but on how he uses the materials of instruction to provide the right 'learning conditions'. The logic is compelling: if you want a particular outcome you must use the right tools — what could be more straightforward? But as Gagné and Briggs are forced to admit:

> Unfortunately, research has not yielded data permitting sweeping generalizations about media . . . Individual differences among learners and among teaching topics are too many and diverse to permit such simple rules for decision-making. Consequently, good judgment must be used in planning just how to accomplish each instructional event for the lesson plan. (ibid., pp. 151-2)

Despite all the sophistication the vital link in the chain is still 'good judgement' and nowhere is there any guide to what that may be. Implicit in the above admission is that it is the complexity of the phenomenon that defeats the researcher. What seems to follow, therefore, is that more powerful research must be needed, so that 'good judgement' can be replaced by hard science; and it is argued, despite this obvious present gap in the chain of decision-making, that the basic systems approach is still viable and that the promise of control will ultimately be fulfilled.

One of the directions in which research has proceeded is to try to match the elaborate taxonomies and hierarchies of objectives and capabilities with taxonomies and hierarchies of the media. One such widely used system (Dale, 1969) bases its hierarchy of media on the notion that certain forms are inherently more difficult to learn from, or are more abstract, than others. The categories, with the most abstract at the top, are:

12. Verbal symbols
11. Visual symbols — signs, stick figures

10. Radio and recordings
 9. Still pictures
 8. Motion pictures
 7. Educational television
 6. Exhibits
 5. Study trips
 4. Demonstrations
 3. Dramatised experiences — plays, puppets; role-playing
 2. Contrived experiences — models, mock-ups; simulations
 1. Direct purposeful experiences.

Anyone familiar with the media cited would regard as absurd this gross classification of, for example, all educational television or all still pictures into homogeneous categories of equal difficulty or abstractness. Any activity, given the attention of highly skilled practitioners, can aspire to a level of sophistication that can in turn simplify and clarify what is complex, or explore the very limits of intricacy or transcendence. Dale's hierarchy only reflects prevailing prejudices and assumptions about the media.

There are underlying reasons why a search for a media taxonomy with a systems-based approach is not viable. First, a media taxonomy is a classification of the media independent of author or audience, something which, I have argued, cannot be logically sustained. Dale's conception is grossly insensitive at the relatively simple level of form; the presumption that any author or audience would automatically be satisfied with his proscription is manifestly wrong. When considerations of content are introduced, the problems are magnified. Secondly, the concept of effects which is at the basis of the mechanistic notion of learning, and an important ingredient in systems analysis, cannot be applied to the realm of communication and meaning. Once the transition is made from information to communication one has broken the causal nexus and replaced it with the fluid system of consciousness and understanding. There is only one way in which it is possible to predict the outcome of using a particular medium, and that is if one can ensure beforehand that everyone using it has an identical set of expectations and an identical knowledge of the conventions used. There are a number of systems of communication which rely on this kind of standardisation. Technical and scientific communication are the most obvious examples — plans, maps, charts, diagrams and graphs depend to a very high degree on systems of notation with standardised meanings. But even here,

Figure 14

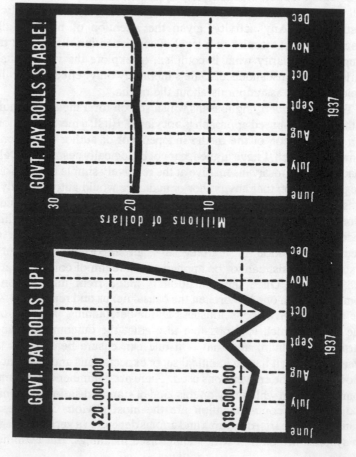

Source: Darrell Huff, *How to Lie with Statistics* (Victor Gollancz, London, 1969).

standardisation usually leaves certain areas of decision-making unspecified and it is these which present problems. For example, in the construction of graphs (Figure 14), convention states that the horizontal axis should be used for the independent variable and the vertical axis for the dependent variable, but does not state what the scale of each should be. It is possible to arrive at different representations of the same information using the same conventions but different scales, having then to face the question of whether the difference is important or not, to whom, and under what conditions. The answer will depend not on a predetermined principle but on the context of usage, which leads us back to the audience/message and author/message and away from an independent analysis of the message. If this is the case with a very simple and highly standardised form like a graph, how much more so must it be for something as complex and variable as film?

These arguments reveal the emptiness of the systems approach. Control of the learning situation is possible if one controls the conventions of interpretation. If, independently of the particular learning system in question, one ensures that students know the conventions being used and share identical expectations, one can predict the outcome. There is no need for an elaborate vocabulary to plan that kind of instruction. But equally the areas of uncertainty and unpredictability will not become less so simply because one has acquired an elaborate vocabulary.

The emphasis in educational technology tends to be on objectives, hardware and evaluation. These are the three points at which control can be exercised. They are, however, all extraneous to the activity in which the learning takes place. The points of contact — communication and learning — remain elusively out of reach and out of control. The illusion generated by positive evaluation is that all is well; but the evidence (Schramm, 1977) suggests that learning from the media is not basically difficult in any case, and a demonstration that learning has taken place is not very revealing. The quality of that learning remains undetermined. There is a wide range of choices for presentation, using the media available. It is difficult to believe that textbook, slide and tape programmes and film offer identical learning experience. Equally there must be choices within any form which can enhance or detract from that experience. To show that an unwittingly bad choice of medium and poorly executed software still results in learning is to demonstrate that students as an audience want to learn and make the best use of whatever resources are available in order to achieve that end. It does *not* demonstrate that the educator is making the best use of those resources, and it leaves unanswered the question of what constitutes a good or bad media choice.

Direct and Mediated Learning

In an important and seminal paper Jerome Bruner and David Olson proposed a reconceptualisaton of media learning (Bruner and Olson, 1973). They suggest that learning could be classified into three kinds deriving from three modes of experience: direct action, models and symbolic systems. Each, they argue, may 'converge as to the knowledge conveyed, but they diverge as to the skills they assume and develop' (p. 225). The notion of passive learning is rejected.

> Living systems have an integrity of their own; they have commerce with the environment on their own terms, selecting from the environment and building representations of this environment as required for the survival and fulfilment of the individual and the species ... we have a picture of reality that is biased by or coded in terms of our actions on it: knowledge is always mediated or specified through some form of human activity. (Bruner and Olson, pp. 211-12)

This conception of direct action, and its consequences for knowledge, is (as I suggested in the introduction) a fundamental change in epistemology. What is at stake here is a proposition which is not amenable to empirical test and it is important to realise that while it may lead to particular empirical enquiry it cannot itself be the subject of that enquiry. Further, methods of enquiry that owe their origin and rationale to the stimulus–response empiricism which has guided a great deal of educational research are inconsistent and out of place in this changed epistemology (a point that will be developed later).

Direct action, as a mode of experience, and hence learning, needs to be considered in two ways: first (and more obviously) as a means of acquiring information about the world, and secondly (and possibly less obviously) as a means of acquiring information about the activity itself — so we have knowledge of the world and skills for acquiring that knowledge.

Modelling or providing demonstrations as a means of experience is equally a two-part process resulting in the acquisition of knowledge and the development of skills.

Symbolic systems — language, pictures, television and so on — provide the final mode of experience and here too the dual notion of that experience is manifest. There is learning from these symbolic systems and there are the skills necessary for understanding how to read these symbolic systems.

> These media make strong assumptions about the literacy of the learner. The properties of a 'good' explanation, description or portrayal are complex subjects worthy of study in their own right. But to untangle the educational effects of these symbolic systems we again have to differentiate the knowledge of the world conveyed through the system from the skills involved in the mastery of the structure of the medium itself. (ibid., p. 225)

While these sentiments are largely shared by this author there are some points of difference. It is not the media that make assumptions but those who use them. This is part of the general misguided presumption about the integrity of message systems which disguises in this case the conflation of real author with inferred author and real audience with inferred audience. It is also, as I have previously suggested, too readily assumed that the homogeneity of usage enjoyed by language as a symbolic system is shared by all symbolic systems and this can lead to the false presumptions about their educational utility. Finally I question the assumption that the dichotomy of skills and knowledge adequately serves to characterise learning from the media. Even in photography — that most obvious of 'windows on to the world' — the relation is more complex. There are certain senses in which the photograph as object in its own right can be a source of information given the appropriate kind of action. It need not necessarily be a mediating system but in certain audience/message relations it can function as direct experience. There are further subtle relations which affect the status of the media and this means that 'to untangle the educational effects of symbolic systems' we need more than the knowledge/skills dichotomy.

None the less the insights of Bruner and Olson have added rich new dimensions to our consideration of education and they revitalise an older debate which has centred around the relation between reality and how we represent that reality. In particular their ideas have provoked the question whether some of the newer media such as television and film, because of the cognitive skills that are required to 'read' them, actually develop new modes of thinking. McLuhan raised this question originally by pointing to the linear and sequential nature of the written word, arguing that it encouraged linear and sequential thinking. As our society was changing from a literary to an electronic culture, changes would occur in our ways of thinking. More recent investigations, using the kinds of concepts developed above, have tried to investigate the empirical basis, if any, for this hypothesis.

Media Cognition and Learning

The most extensive, imaginative and conceptually developed study along these lines in recent years is Gavriel Salomon's study of the interaction between media cognition and learning (Salomon, 1979). It seems well to illustrate the major strengths and weaknesses of this emerging area of research.

The starting point of Salomon's enquiry is that 'Media's ways of structuring and presenting information — that is, their symbol systems — are media's most important attributes when learning and cognition are considered' (Salomon, p. 216).

Yet again the basic conceptual problems are present: the conflation of audience/message and author/message; the presumptions of message integrity; the media acting as secondary experience, 'structuring and presenting information'. However, despite these obvious short-comings, it is possible to ignore the conceptual problems and view the research in a much simpler way, as examining the relation between the conventions of film-making, cognition and learning.

By using a series of experimental studies in which children were exposed to different filmic presentations of information, Salomon is able, within the limits of the experimental methods used, to show that there are indeed measurable relations between, on the one hand, the conventions of film-making used, and on the other the knowledge and skills acquired and developed.

In general this means that choices of media are not irrelevant and that the method by which information is encoded in a message influences learning. An experienced film or television director might be forgiven at this stage for saying 'So what's new?' but given the history of educational media research this is indeed new. Ever since film-making began, the long shot, fade, blur, close-up, zoom, etc., have been developed with a view to enhancing and refining the meaning of film experience. Educational research, in its early stages, began with the simple undifferentiated concept of 'media'. Thus

Salomon's close attention to what he calls the symbolic system of film represents a quantum leap in sensitivity and an affirmation to film-makers that their techniques, developed in the isolation of practice, do make some difference to our experiences of film. This may cause those audio-visual specialists who have come into the area from a background in educational psychology or hardware to pay more attention to the craft of film-making; there is certainly a general lesson in that.

Salomon's research is addressed to the educational research community, not the practising teacher, and may prove largely inaccessible to the latter, who, often hampered by an inadequate knowledge of statistics, may find it difficult to understand the research, let alone translate it into practice. This means that the educator is effectively excluded from the debate; the researchers are left talking to each other.

There is a more fundamental reason, concerned with the very heart of the research design, why the kind of research conducted by Salomon may prove difficult to apply in practice. I have commented earlier in this chapter on the changed epistemological conception of learning which guides Salomon's work, but it is still the case that his methods of investigation echo an earlier epistemology — that of extreme empiricism and positivism. Despite the fact that perception is treated conceptually as an active process, in the experimental design it is treated as passive; the film is regarded as acting on the children. This leads to an ambiguity in interpretation of results because it is not clear what or who is acting on what or whom!

Experiments are not socially neutral, even if the experimenter treats them as such. The subjects of experiments come to them from other social encounters — attending a class, having coffee, playing in the playground. From the subjects' point of view and from the perspective of the newer ideas about learning these are *actions* that people engage in. Subjects in Salomon's experiments were not told at the time what they were supposed to learn of the content of the film or what specific skills they were to try to acquire. Only afterwards, in another context, were they tested for *effects*. The obvious contradiction in this approach is disturbing. It is as if only indirect covert learning is important. From the point of view of the subjects taking part (in what to them is another kind of social encounter) there is something basically underhand, even deceitful, in the experimenter's refusal to tell them what he is interested in. I have personal experience of this. I was once invited by some architecture students to help them interpret the results of tests that were supposed to determine which of a number of different representations of buildings gave people most information about those buildings. A sample of the public, who were told nothing of the real purpose of the exercise, took part. Afterwards I asked the subjects if any of them had viewed the exercise as a test of their own ability, and three-quarters of them said that this was how they saw it. It was, of course, the representations, not they, that were being tested; but everything about the occasion, and the way it was structured, pointed to the kind of test situation with which the subjects identified one set of actions, rather than to a situation where their advice was being actively sought which would have been favoured by a different set of actions. The effect this had on their answers became apparent when they discovered the true purpose of the encounter, and many indicated that, had they known, they would have answered differently.

Salomon's studies are similarly of limited value. It is inconsistent to describe learning as active, and then proceed to treat subjects as if they are merely acted on. In most teaching situations students are given some framework for action — that is, they are told what is expected of them. This happens both overtly through what has been said or written by teaching staff, and covertly through informal channels and implicit rules — what has come to be known as the hidden curriculum (Snyder, 1973). Incidental learning obviously takes place, and sometimes can be more important for student success than the manifest subject matter of a course; but what interests teachers in the main are those aspects of learning that they can influence and direct. It may be the case, particularly with young children, that some of the purposes behind a particular activity are left unexplained, but it is usual to give some framework even if it is restricted to the immediate task in hand.

Perhaps the best way of viewing Salomon's contribution is in terms of the hidden curriculum. If, as his experiments suggest, children's cognitive skills are influenced in their development by particular media conventions then it is time to ask very probing questions about the hidden curriculum. How much of this learning should be allowed to remain outside direct influence?

Underlying this is a more profound question about the nature of the skills involved. An assumption that runs through all the work reviewed in this chapter is that the media are channels for carrying information. Olson, Bruner and Salomon have sensitised us to the relation between media-viewing skills on the one hand and the information the media convey on the other, but the media are perceived throughout as having a monolithic function of conveying information. It follows from this view that there could be only two basic questions: what structure of transformation do the media impose on the information, and what skills are required to reconstitute or transform the message so produced into knowledge of the world? It appears as though there is only a finite set of skills with a limited set of consequences for our modes of thought and apprehension of the world. This view will be challenged in the next and subsequent chapters.

Learning, Schema and Objectification

It remains for me to integrate the emerging conception of learning with the basic concepts of this book. The notion of skill must closely correspond to the concept of schema. This is acknowledged by Salomon (p. 75) who takes a narrower view of schema than that proposed by Neisser (1976) in that he is concerned only with schema that internalise symbolic processes, whereas Neisser is concerned with all modes of action, symbolic and non-symbolic alike. None the less they both see the functional basis of schemata as being a kind of anticipatory framework. It is not a precise conception; any attempt to pin it down in terms of neurological correlates or definite behavioural outcomes is bound to fail. The concept does enable us to deal with and describe that aspect of learning which is directed by the knowledge and expectations of the learner, something over which the instructor has no direct influence and which thwarts the hopes of those seeking an unrealistic control of learning.

The concept of objectification does not find a readily available niche in the theories described and its significance for learning will be developed in the chapters to come, where its importance both in the construction of messages and in the understanding of messages will be explored.

The overriding conclusion of both this chapter and Chapter 4 is that developments in the use of visual communication must proceed along two fronts. Careful attention needs to be devoted to the processes of message construction but equally we must focus on the skills of understanding these messages. Each learner brings a range of skills to bear on the educational message. These are bound to be drawn in the main from common cultural knowledge of such things, which will also be shared by the author. But there are, within each encounter, idiosyncratic elements which cannot be controlled and which should realistically limit expectations. Despite the claims of systems-based approaches to learning, there can be no formal set of procedures which guarantee learning outcomes.

6 THE PHOTOGRAPH

Introduction

How do we become conscious and articulate about the commonplace? That is the problem posed to us by the photograph. All around us in our homes, in the streets, in the pages of countless magazines and books we find an endless procession of photographic images. There is no field of human activity which has not found some use for the photograph. The skyline of New York, the Taj Mahal, the war in Vietnam, the agonies of concentration camps, the atom bomb, the surface of the moon and a parade of famous people are all known to us through the photograph. Family life is enshrined in the photograph album. This picture-making system is so rich in its offerings that we do not pause to reflect upon its nature; we are seduced by the content to such a degree that we are left speechless about the form.

When John Locke, the father of empiricism, said in 1690 that the mind was a blank slate on which experience writes he gave us the philosophical metaphor for the photograph which followed 150 years later. It was the desire to record accurately the objects in the world, which had proved so elusive and difficult for the painter, that led to the invention of photography; and the history of the development of photographic technology can be seen as a constant search for more effective ways of achieving fidelity with nature. It is one of the great technological achievements of empiricism. Content is supreme. Photography is the champion of empiricism: the view that the objects in the world are the only source of knowledge.

If all we had to say about a photograph could be said with reference to its subject matter, we would be missing a great deal. In this chapter there will be much to say about the relation of the photograph to its maker and user.

I shall begin with an examination of the way in which the medium of photography imposes particular kinds of restraints on the photographer and how, through skilful choices, these limitations have been transcended. I will then examine how these choices affect the epistemological status of photographs. We will then be in a position to start the discussion on the educational uses of photographs.

As we have seen, there is no exact correspondence between a

93

particular medium and its pedagogic value. This generates problems in deciding to devote a chapter to a particular medium. We will not in this chapter exhaust the pedagogic value of photographs but will begin the process of unfolding the potentiality of all illustrative material with some emphasis on the peculiar cultural value we attribute to photographs.

The Myth and Metaphor of Transparency

Photographs tend to imply a metaphor of transparency; they suggest by their very closeness to nature that they are a window into a part of the world. The photographer does not seem to impose himself between us and the content. I referred to this in Chapter 4 as a way in which the inferred author is suppressed, creating an audience/message relation where the status of the photograph appears to slip into the realm of information. The mechanical basis of photography seems to deny any role to the photographer. As the early photographers described the process, it is light, not the artist, which paints the picture. This places the photographer in a subtly different role to that of other communicators. The areas of choice are different. A painter, for example, can choose a whole range of techniques of painting and he can innovate with new styles. (It is partly on the basis of style that one can distinguish between a Rembrandt, a van Gogh and a Matisse; the artist, if he chooses and has the ability, can use every stroke of his brush to mark the image with his own identity.) Realism in art was a deliberate and difficult choice to make. The suppression of individuality for the sake of optical fidelity involved the slow accumulation of skills over many generations, a hard-won battle. Ironically, the basis of optical realism, as its greatest exponents discovered, lies as much in the eye of the beholder as on the surface of the canvas (Gombrich, 1960).

What became a disciplined choice by painters of extraordinary talent is now the casual accomplishment of the most untutored photographer. It is therefore inevitable that excellence among photographers should develop in directions other than the endless repetition of optical realism, which by its mechanical directness makes the photographer seem superfluous. Equally if we are to develop some sense of the uses of photographs in education it is necessary to move beyond the simple photographic trick of realism.

It would be misleading to suggest that photographers have always fought the impersonal quality of photographs. The seeming ability of the photograph to speak for itself must be a strong ingredient of any use of photography for reportage whether of a scientific, military, forensic or documentary kind.

The photographer is discreetly invisible; he seems not to intrude between the information and the user. But in these forms as in all others the hand of the photographer is there even if we do not notice it.

The way the photographer can be made visible is by considering the range of choices available to him. The choices are literally infinite. Even if he were locked in a room, his choice of angles of shot, composition and content would be alarmingly large. But photographers do not point their cameras at everything. They select; and while we may be seduced by the impression of an open window we should never forget that out of an infinite universe of possible windows only one has been opened for us. In other words there is a conscious, purposeful controlling agent behind every photograph, and if we are to look towards a more articulate understanding of the value of photographs then we must ask the question: why? Why did the photographer make that choice at that particular moment? In asking that question we will be led to a consideration of the relationship between the photographer and his subject.

The Photographer's Choice

When Daguerre announced his great invention to the public in the summer of 1839, he explained how it worked but not really what it was for . . . What the daguerreotype was in fact used for was recording the faces of millions of people. Of the countless thousands of daguerreotype that survive, not one in a hundred shows a building or a waterfall or a street scene; the rest is an endless parade of ancestors. (Szarkowski, 1973, p. 14)

From the earliest days the photographers' choices have never been neutral or simple. Caught in a web of expectations sometimes of their own making but more often woven by the society of which they were a part, the photographer developed a sense of his craft, its problems and potentials. The preoccupation with portraiture was a particularly problematic choice in the early days of photography because of the slowness of the plates. Subjects had to sit, often with head clamped, for a minute or more to ensure a sharp image. Inanimate objects would have been much easier subjects but it is an indication of the importance of social pressures in determining photographic preferences that photographers made choices which strained the technical limitations of their equipment rather than work comfortably within these limitations. But right from the start there was more to the activity than simply pointing the camera at the desired subject. Even if photography was new, the art of picture-making was not. Having one's portrait painted was a matter of high status, indicating wealth and privilege. It is not surprising therefore that the early photographers should carry on the conventions of a prior age; the subject was organised in such a way as to result in a photograph that would look like a painted picture. Folds in drapery, lighting, props, posture and expression all conspired to associate the photograph with its hand-made forerunner. It is possible to see this as pretension, a kind of mimicry. It is perhaps more likely to be the ingenuous initial reaction to a new form whose working methods had not yet been established.

In our own time, television production still bears the traces of its origins in the crafts of film-making, journalism and radio production. The inappropriateness of applying the conventions of painting to photography soon became apparent. If the painter overlooks something because his schema does not initiate a search for it, it does not appear on the canvas. Thus optical realism for the painter is partly a matter of personal expectations. If the photographer does not notice something as he clicks the shutter, the ever faithful optics of the camera certainly do. This leads to an epistemological crisis. Most of us, even if we have only taken snapshots, have faced, sinkingly, that moment of truth when the pictures come back from processing and the evidence before us conflicts with our memory and expectation of what should have been there. Typically, what we find is that our subject, contrary to our impression at the time, occupies a tiny space in a large background full of all sorts of things that we failed to notice at the time. There are many other problems engendered by the obvious difference between the way we look at the world and the way we look at photographs. What is invisible to us in the world cannot be avoided in a photograph. The idea that looking at objects in pictures is the same as looking at objects in the world cannot be true. Optics dictate that the information is the same. Perception dictates that the experience is different. The photographer faces this problem constantly and the remarkable fact, which has gone unnoticed by those outside the profession, is that he develops a way of seeing which is quite different from ordinary perception and which enables him to judge what he sees through the viewfinder in terms of the eventual print. He scans the view for those features that will enhance or detract from the final product. Looking through the viewfinder he is engaged in an act of transformation. The schema developed by photographers in order to accomplish this transformation turns the eye into a new kind of instrument of judgement. Photographic seeing is a kind of perception unknown before the camera. If there was any need to prove that different media can give rise to the development of specific cognitive skills then photographic seeing is that proof.

Photographic seeing is not a limited or finite skill; the features which are of importance to one photographer may not necessarily be so to another. It is a multi-faceted skill which has been developed to serve a wide range of purposes. It is tempting at this point to introduce a number of photographs by way of example, but for reasons that are central to the thesis of this book, that temptation will be resisted. To introduce an example at this point in the argument would suggest that it is possible to infer reliably from message to author. There is no doubt that I could give a plausible example which would seem to link the audience/message relation directly with the author's purpose, but to do so would gloss over the very real distinction between the audience/message relation and the author/message relation. If the reader were not aware of different photographic purposes then pointing to specific photographs as demonstrations of any particular purpose would involve the use of objectification rather than evidence as a basis of the argument. Accordingly, specific photographs and their relation to the reader will be examined later. What can be done in order to give some insight into the variety of photographic purposes is to look at statements made by photographers about how they regard their art.

Up to and including the instant of exposure, the photographer is working in an undeniably subjective way. By his choice of technical approach (which is a tool of emotional control), by his selection of the subject matter to be held within the confines of his negative area, and by his decision as to the exact, climactic instant of exposure, he is blending the variables of interpretation into an emotional whole which will be a basis for the formation of opinion by the viewing public.

It is the responsibility of the photographer-journalist to take his assignment and examine it — to search with intelligence for the frequently intangible truth; and then very carefully (and sometimes very rapidly) work to bring his insight, as well as the physical characteristics of the subject, to his finished pictures. (W. Eugene Smith, 1948)

This account by a photo-journalist reveals some interesting aspects of the author/message relation. The moment of exposure could not be more specific, more particular — it is a particular object frozen at a specific point in time; and yet the photographer sees it as standing for 'an emotional whole', 'an intangible truth'. The photograph for all its particularity is regarded by the photographer as offering us a generalisation. He imbues it not with its obvious and manifest literal meaning but with a figurative meaning. In this case the figurative device used is called synedoche, where the part stands for the whole, the particular stands for the general. I will have a great deal to say about such figurative devices as we proceed, but at this stage we are dealing only with a photographer's assertion that the photograph can fulfil that kind of purpose, and it is clear from this example that the purpose is unashamedly rhetorical. Thus the photographer believes that his *constructed* audience forms its opinions by viewing the photograph. Whether these claims are justified with reference to a real audience is not at issue here but there can be little doubt that the photographers' belief in them enables us to begin to understand the kind of choices made by this famous photo-journalist.

An earlier photographer reflecting different preoccupations and celebrating the invention of the hand-held camera said about photographing urban landscapes:

In order to obtain pictures by means of the hand camera it is well to choose your subject, regardless of figures, and carefully study the lines and lighting. After having determined upon these watch the passing figures and await the moment in which everything is in balance; that is, satisfies the eye. This often means hours of patient waiting. My picture 'Fifth Avenue Winter' is the result of a three hours' stand during a fierce snow-storm on February 22nd 1893, awaiting the proper moment. (Alfred Stieglitz, 1897)

Here the particular is observed but the guiding principles are formal and aesthetic. Unlike the painter who can organise the elements on the canvas, the photographer intent on similar purposes must be patient and allow time to compose the picture. Once again the specificity of the picture is displaced and the photographer is telling us that his choice of the decisive moment must be judged in terms of criteria not present within the particularity of the picture.

Some photographers have followed a purist line with respect to their medium and have explored with great intensity the medium's ability to particularise; in this they have discovered yet another kind of displacement away from literal meaning:

> Photography is basically too honest a medium for recording superficial aspects of a subject. It searches out the actor behind the make-up and exposes the contrived, the trivial, the artificial, for what they really are. But the camera's innate honesty can hardly be considered a limitation of the medium since it bars only that kind of subject matter that properly belongs to the painter. On the other hand it provides the photographer with a means of looking deeply into the nature of things, and presenting his subjects in terms of their basic reality. It enables him to reveal the essence of what lies before his lens with such clear insight that the beholder may find the recreated image more real and comprehensible than the actual object. (Edward Weston, 1943)

The specific is transformed into its essence. If these considerations seem to be remote from education Weston's final sentence should be re-examined. It contains a recognisable pedagogic purpose related to his constructed audience.

What all these examples show is that photographers have entertained the idea that photographic meanings can go beyond the simple mechanical act of recording the visible form of objects in the world. Not all photographers are as articulate or decisive — or as well known — as the three I have quoted, and between them they do not exhaust the range of purposes and choices made by photographers. What I hope is clear is that a range of possibilities for decision-making is part of every photographic act. The product of that act — the photograph — is never just a window. The difference between a great photographer and the ordinary practitioner is that the photographic seeing of the master is constantly renewing itself and displays acute control and judgement; the ordinary practitioner learns the conventional options and follows these. But at whatever level, there are always choices and they reflect preoccupations that go beyond the photograph itself. Whether we are aware of these or not they do have a central bearing on the epistemological status of any photograph.

Paradoxically the things that generate meaning for a photographer in the photographic act are all those things he excludes. Photographers, by framing an aspect of the visible world, categorise it. In most instances the inclusions and exclusions are governed by conventions that, because of their widespread use, are barely noticeable, but because the photographic act is informed by preconceptions and is never an act of innocence the meaning of the image, to its maker at least, is much richer than its simple content.

The 'stand-for' relation which the photographer generates always has a certain figurative quality. Even if the stated purpose of the photographer is literal — for example, taking a photograph of a house — there is such a wide range of choices with respect to that task that some external criteria must guide the choice. Should it be photographed from the front, back or side? From oblique angle, the air or inside? A common strategy is to photograph the front because it is a common architectural convention to define the quality and kind of house from its frontal aspect. That in itself presumes a conception of 'front'. In photographic terms it means that the front stands for the whole of the house. There is always a sense in which more is implied than is present. How crude or subtle, simple or complex this additional meaning can be will depend on the skill and originality of the photographer and his conception of the photographic act.

The Photograph's Context

We do not expect photographers to stand by their product and explain it to us. It leaves their influence and moves into an intermediate domain where it is subject to editorial decisions. In this way it is transformed. The meaning in the author/message relation cannot be assumed to find its way unaltered into the audience/message relation. The new context of the photograph requires a new analysis of meaning. Books, magazines, newspapers, billboards, galleries and photograph albums are all possible contexts for photographs. Each gives a nudge to the viewer — perhaps a helping hand to guide the act of looking. Each tends to be a venue for particular kinds of photographs, though the boundaries are indistinct; it would be surprising to find a Playgirl of the Month in a family album or a snapshot in an art gallery. That these and others seem to be recognisable as distinct genres is a point worth considering. Like the style of the artist, something of the basis of choices which determined a particular photographic act is perspicuous in the photograph (provided one has had prior experience of photographs within particular areas of choice).

Figure 15 is a snapshot, Figure 16 a newspaper photograph and Figure 17 a photograph used in an advertisement. Each in its own context has a particular status and information value. The snapshot depends on a consuming interest in the particular family, representing as it does a moment in the personal history of that family. The newspaper photograph also represents a moment — but it is a public moment; the family is observed by an outsider. That is part of the defining characteristic of photo-journalism. The advertisement is also public, but in a different sense. The family is simulated, idealised, flattered, but we accept this as part of the rhetorical role of advertising. In each case there is a different implied epistemological status: personal knowledge in the first, public detached knowledge in the second and plausible fiction in the third.

Figure 15: Snapshot

Now let us suppose that these illustrations were to be used in a sociological text on kinship relations in Western society. How would each differ in relation to the purpose of the book? Assuming the origins and original purpose of each are intelligible to the audience of the book

Figure 16: Newspaper Photograph

Source: *The Age*, Melbourne.

in which they are reproduced, we can speculate at this point on the meaning that would be generated by the audience/message relation. The snapshot lends itself to a kind of authenticity. Here is a real family

Figure 17: Advertising Photograph

Source: By permission of Danepak Ltd.

photographed willingly in its own surroundings; the basis of any point in the text — however abstract — would seem to be drawn from an awareness of the particular and personal nature of family life when placed alongside the snapshot. The photograph can be seen not only as representing a particular family but also as representative of the concept of 'family' as a personal experience. It is as if this picture taken out of its original context points each of us to an awareness in our own life of the photograph album as a symbol of family identity. Its particular and personal origins are transformed into a symbol.

The newspaper photograph, if used, offers an altogether different conception of the family. It is a detached view — the photographer and his subjects are not related. He is observing them, not participating in their rituals. The message is potentially either an impartial, scientifically detached view or a committed, but involved, point of view. In either instance the institutional nature of the family is represented. Whereas with the snapshot there is a suggestion that we should know at first hand the individuals depicted in order to relate appropriately to the photograph, the press photograph does not require such a reaction. We can empathise with or understand this family through a shared conception of the nature of the family but we do not need to know them personally. Moreover, there is an added narrative dimension. They have been photographed for a reason — something has happened to bring them under public gaze. The incident, whatever it may have been, has catalysed the change from private to public domain. These levels of meaning make the press photograph a symbol of a different kind.

The advertising photograph is the product of a stage-managed 'event'. It is a fiction. The use of this photograph in the text on kinship would set up very different expectations, and of all the photographs this one is in a certain sense the easiest to relate to. There is no standard of veridicality against which to judge meaning, only the standards of plausibility. If the people and situation depicted seem unreal, we can reject them; there is no obligation as with the snapshot or press photograph to attempt to match one's world view with the world of the photograph. This provides an altogether more fluid and controversial frame of reference. The photograph could be an ideal, a stereotype, a reflection or a lie.

The three photographs of roughly the same content can lend themselves to very different meanings. This whole analysis presumes that the audience will approach the photographs with a conception of the author consistent with the descriptions I have offered. Further it presumes that the focus of attention will be on the epistemological status of the photographs not, for example, on the social status of the family or the ideological significance of using these kinds of images. These latter alternatives are possible audience/message relations which would draw on different aspects of the photographs and would organise the available information using different schemata. In all cases objectification provides a powerful reinforcement to the main-tenance of the meaning derived.

If the origins of these photographs are assumed to be consistent with my descriptions, and the reader is familiar with the differences which are implied by snapshot, press and advertising photograph, then the meanings *appear* to come from the photographs themselves; but in fact, neither the source of the photographs, nor the different cultural settings implied, are actually part of the photograph. They are part of common knowledge that I am presuming to share with the reader. If, as might happen with children or members of other cultures, the essential knowledge is not there, the differences in meaning, critical as they are, would simply not be there either. I may perhaps be presuming a degree of uniformity in responsiveness to different institutions, and a qualitative assessment of these differences, which might not exist even within our own culture. There may well be among my readers those who would wish to insist that a photograph, no matter what its origins, is perceived as a simple record of what is there in the world, in which case authorship is suppressed (or perhaps of no consequence) and the photograph is examined with a schema appropriate for information, not communication. Thus the myth of transparency can overshadow inferred authorship and the distinction between information and communication becomes clouded — even disappears, diffused into a vague notion of 'information'.

It would be very easy to fall into the trap of making assumptions about the way an audience would interpret the photographs. The comparisons I have made are only a possible, if plausible, inter-pretation of the outcomes of using any of them, but it serves to show something of the problems involved in using photographs in educational material.

Photographs in Texts

I have up till now not questioned the legitimacy of having a photograph or any other illustration in a text. From the discussion in Chapter 5 on the relation between media and learning it is clear that there is a general belief that the media are worthwhile — but nobody is quite sure why. It is an interesting phenomenon of our culture that despite the absence of any substantial theory to guide choices of visual material there is no shortage of illustrated texts at all levels. It is, however, not clear what specific educational value illustrations in texts may have.

Texts are not the only, nor necessarily the most important, context for illustrations but they provide a useful location for discussing the uses to which illustrations might be put. Most attempts at developing a description of pictorial material in education are either quasi-semantic (Knowlton, 1966) or morphological (Fleming, 1967; Twyman, 1979). The former provides a system for classifying the presumed logical relationship between any illustration and what it is supposed to stand for. This is the kind of analysis that I have undertaken with respect to the photographs of the family. However, Knowlton's classification is too crude and provides at best a limited set of logical categories. It fails completely to catch any of the figurative, epistemological or cultural nuances that are potentially there. The greatest problems of such attempts are due to the fact that they proceed from an analysis of the message, not of the author/message or audience/message relation. We are therefore left with the question of where the meaning is properly to be located: with the message, the author or the audience? In actuality the meaning is located in the relation set up by whoever is conducting the classification and presumed to be the same in any other context. Even when we have arrived at such a description we are still faced with the problem of the educational role of the illustration.

The morphological approach is equally flawed as it is based on the assumption that form and function are somehow related (without actually specifying how). It is assumed that a formal description of the elements of an illustration in terms of line, shape, medium, etc., will be of some pedagogic value. However this too stops short of providing a basis for making decisions.

There are hopeful signs of a more direct approach in some recent work (Duchastel, 1978; Duchastel and Waller, 1979). Duchastel develops a functional approach to illustration which if used appropriately has great promise. He distinguishes between three categories of purposes for which illustrations either are used or could be used: attentional, explicative and retentional.

Attentional illustrations he defines as those that 'make the text more interesting to pick up, more interesting to browse through and more interesting to read . . . An attentional illustration then is one which need only provoke the eye' (Duchastel, 1978, p. 37).

Explicative illustrations 'explain a given aspect of the topic being presented or they add something which is not clearly expressible in words' (ibid., p. 38).

Retentional illustrations are of a less obvious kind. Their role is based on the established fact that the human capacity for memorising pictures is less degradable than memory for verbal information (Paivio, 1975) and therefore illustrations

are presumed to act somewhat as do section headings, that is to say, they form a conceptual plan of the subject matter for the learner, although an iconic plan rather than a verbal one . . . During later recall, the student can initially retrieve from memory the iconic representations of the topics which were presented in the text, and through these he or she gains immediate access to their verbal representations. (Duchastel, 1978, p. 38)

Duchastel is careful to point out that these categories are not mutually exclusive and an illustration may fulfil more than one role. He goes on to suggest rather rashly that the best person to choose illustrations is the instructional designer because 'he is generally more cognizant of learning theory than the author, and more concerned with the effects of the text on student learning than is the graphic designer' (ibid., p. 39). We have seen in Chapter 5 that a knowledge of learning theory is not a very useful guide to learning practice and it is interesting to see the term 'effects' being used. A close examination of Duchastel's description of the three roles reveals that he believes that illustrations 'make', 'provoke', 'explain' and 'act'. We are by now familiar with this false animation of the inanimate — the invocation of the active message stamping itself on the consciousness (or unconsciousness) of the learner. As we have seen there is a long history of treating messages as if they were active agents and we have also seen how that generates a contradiction particularly when using a theory of active, not passive, perception. However, if one regards Duchastel's functions not as ways of describing what pictures do but as ways of describing the audience/message relation then we have the beginnings of a working taxonomy for at least a few of the potential audience/message relations that occur in an educational context.

It is worth examining in detail Duchastel's view that the categories are not exclusive. This is not because pictures in themselves are inherently flexible and multipurpose in the manner of a boy scout's pen-knife, but because the relations they can be part of are extremely flexible. To say that illustration's three roles can overlap is an elegant way of admitting that one's control over those relations is slight. A better way of formulating the question about the relation between illustration and learning is to ask what students are to use illustration for. This shifts the onus of action on to the student and away from the illustration which is of course the passive partner in the relation. In effect the question becomes: What schema do we want the student to use? and underlying that question must be: How do we ensure that the student applies an appropriate schema? To answer each of these questions we need to turn, in this and in following chapters, to a detailed examination of the three audience/message relations.

Attentional Relation

This is a common and debased relation which is an artefact of our pictorially saturated culture. It stems from a superficial use of pictures and in itself encourages the false belief that seeing is sensory and that pictures are simple and self-evident. Duchastel unwittingly captures the banality of the relation in his attempt to describe so-called attentional illustrations as ones 'which need only provoke the eye' (ibid., p. 37).

It may seem out of place in this context to strike a moral tone, but there is a point where seduction becomes prostitution; and that point is reached with illustrations when they are merely there to provide sensory titillation. Regrettably the demands of the market place have developed those skills of prostitution to a high art. The client is the fickle page-flicker who has to be lured, whose attention must be caught, in as short a time as it takes to turn the page. It is not a very subtle art and does not encourage the development of sophisticated schemata.

A common assumption among analysts of advertising, which is basically attentional (Barthes, 1964; Millum, 1975; Leymore, 1975; Key, 1973; Goffman, 1979; Williamson, 1978), is that there are at least two levels if not more to the meanings of advertisements. Not one of these analysts considers that there is a vast difference between the theory-laden searching schemata of the analyst and the simplistic glance of the idly curious. A further fallacy which is dragged into this divination is that the hidden or 'deeper' meaning (as it is sometimes portentously called) is somehow more powerful than the surface meaning. The notion of the unconscious (whether Freudian, Jungian or some pastiche thereof) is invoked as the process by which this 'deep meaning' passes unnoticed by our critical conscious faculties directly into the mind, there to weave its inexorable and irresistible spell, so that the idly curious have no defence against this assault on their will. The tendency to assume that covert or incidental learning is in some respects more powerful or important than overt learning is even present in comitted empiricists such as Salomon (see Chapter 5).

It should be very clear that this hidden influence is usually believed to take place as a consequence of the correctness of the theory being used in performing the analysis. The analyst does not really need proof because the powerful schemata deployed in the analysis naturally objectify the 'discovered' meaning so that the analyst can claim that the meaning is there in the message. If other analysts cannot see it they are either not looking carefully enough or looking for the wrong things. This is a very serious fallacy — it does not constitute a proof and negates the value of a great deal of semiotic enquiry;

moreover it does not give us a basis for understanding the role that these publicity images play. Far from being subversively powerful it is possible that they blunt sensibility by their sheer quantity and repetitiveness. To put the matter very straightforwardly, the theory of perception developed in these pages asserts that a glance is just a glance, no more, no less. The information available to the eye depends on how long an image is scanned. A glance of a fraction of a second cannot absorb consciously or unconsciously the same information that five minutes' penetrating scrutiny will uncover, especially if that scrutiny is informed by a highly articulate theory. The theory does not need to be true, only believable. Objectification provides all the 'proof' necessary.

In education this tends to encourage a covert style of media usage. The student is not told why a particular illustration is used, for that would destroy its potency. The spell must be cast unknown to the learner.

Illustrations fulfilling an attentional role are meant to motivate the reader, no more. They make the text more interesting to pick up, more interesting to browse through, and more interesting to read.

The resemblance to love potions and their supposed effects is uncanny!

Perhaps there is room for magic in education but it can take a different, less furtive form. Illustrations can be the subject of fascination but it is a fascination that flows from an open acknowledgement of the magical skills of the picture-maker. Photographs of the unique, the exotic, the unusual, have this fascination precisely because we assume action by someone especially privileged or gifted — a traveller perhaps, or someone with an ability to capture the decisive moment or see the world anew. However, these images do not merely 'provoke the eye', they enrich our experience and they do so not because of their content but because of our understanding of the special skills or privileges that made them possible. It is as photographs that we enjoy them, not as sources of 'secondary experience'. They are there in their own right, and not as mere channels of information. Our attempt to identify with the person who took them provides the fascination; if a photograph seems in some way exceptional it is because we infer it to be the product of an exceptional action. Such a photograph in a book might imply by association that the book too shares this exceptional quality. It is attentional because it does not match expectations but it leads to much more than a glance. The magic is that of exceptional human achievement, not trivialised, debased or prostituted. Distinguishing between the exceptional and the merely slick is sometimes difficult — particularly if some insight into the necessary skills is a prerequisite — but there is no doubting the experience. A rich overlay of new figurative meaning accompanies the recognition of the exceptional, whereas the slick only gives rise to cliche.

I am extremely concerned about the quality of our visual thought. No long-term objective in that direction is served by gimmicks designed to attract the eye. In the long term they merely distract and inhibit the development of thought. Thus I take a very guarded view of the use of so-called 'attentional illustrations'. They embody far too much of the shrill cry of the market place which does not belong in education. It should not be concluded as a consequence of this view that illustrations should not be used to enrich and enliven the process of education but to do that requires a reciprocity between illustration and text. As described by Duchastel the 'attentional role' is unidirectional. Having been seduced by the illustration one moves on to the text, never to return to the illustration. I agree that the illustration may be the first thing that is noticed by a reader, but in moving from illustration to text the reader should be directed back to the illustration so that its value in the totality of the process of communication can be understood.

Despite the endless production of pictures in our culture most of them are used in this superficial 'attentional role'. It is therefore likely that *unless the context in which they are to be used offers sufficient guidance as to their use, most students will presume that they have an attentional role and will therefore treat them as only incidentally relevant to learning*. I offer this as a tentative generalisation which has some relevance to the practical use of illustrations in texts. It is unlikely that anything achieved in education will, in the short term, influence our culture. As I pointed out in Chapter 4, the education of vision takes place outside the classroom. The schemata developed for the apprehension of pictures will be no more sophisticated than the demands of the culture. People do not generally require skills for which there is no use. Thus 'attentional' illustrations occupy a quite different and antithetical role to the other two possibilities. It is not simply another role but one which is unfortunately dominant and more importantly a barrier to the explicative or retentional uses of pictures. It is superficial and undemanding whereas the other uses are intellectually taxing. It is in this mindless category that we find most photographs, their role being reinforced by our knowledge of the brevity of the mechanical act that produced them. It would be interesting (though outside our scope here) to trace the origins of this style of looking from the dramatic intentions of artists in pre-photographic times through modern publicity, propaganda and press images. Somewhere within that history sustained rhetoric gave way to the quick effect. Pressure of deadlines and the ephemeral quality of the product must have contributed. The audience also saw yesterday's marvel turn into today's wrapping paper, and worse: the increasing volume of material on the newsstands makes each individual item intrinsically less important — less valuable. This is the milieu of the attentional illustration and it is in contrast to its disposable character that we turn in the next chapters to the other roles of illustration.

7 THE DRAWING

Introduction

There is always a problem when discussing visual communication of deciding on what basis to subdivide the discussion of its uses. I have repeatedly criticised the notion that the media of execution provide a sound basis for construction of a taxonomy: with reservations (which will continue), I have opted for a functional classification. There is, however, an historical handicap in a functional classification; although there are affinities in style, school and influence throughout the visual arts, there are, as we have already seen with respect to photography, quite distinct traditions which are to some extent exclusive to any particular medium. The technical quality of any medium means that there are specific skills associated with its mastery, and there is also a tendency for certain media to be more closely assoicated with some particular functions rather than others. For example, if we wanted to know how someone looked we would nowadays ask to see a photograph. In particular, photography has acquired supremacy over painting or drawing. These last still carry connotations of prestige that photography has never ousted or bettered but photography has verisimilitude and a kind of truth on its side that the hand-made object cannot match. It is also a more economical image-making process.

There is, then, a tendency to associate particular forms with particular types of content. This also has the consequence among practitioners of encouraging the development of conventions which elaborate the ways in which the medium deals with a particular type of content; for example, throughout most of the history of film the dominant use to which it has been put is as a means for telling stories. It is not surprising therefore that most of the conventions of film-making are narrative conventions; and when applied to non-narrative subjects, such as science, film-makers are prone to convert the subject matter into a story (Jones *et al.*, 1978). More subtly perhaps the context in which a medium is used influences the expectations of its use. The BBC has gained a reputation for news programmes, but the producers of such programmes insist on the importance of entertainment values in their production of these programmes (Schlesinger, 1978).

112

These factors do not make for easy classification. For purposes of presentation it is easier to focus on specific media that at least have a tangible set of procedures and traditions in common, but ultimately the only sensible classification for education is one based on function and revolves around the question of what, in any particular instance, we would like a student to use an illustration for. Though this chapter will focus on those functions to which drawing is particularly suited, I will also continue the examination of photography begun in the last chapter.

Explication and Drawing

Continuing our examination of functional categories, we will examine in this chapter part of a subdivision of so-called explicative illustrations. Duchastel and Waller give a brief account of a content analysis of Open University texts which was undertaken with a view to analysing the specific role of illustrations and in particular it tried to answer the question 'What do illustrations do that prose cannot do as well?' (Duchastel and Waller, 1979, p. 21).

Before examining their findings in detail it is necessary to make two qualifications. First, they presume that the illustrations are active. It is what they 'do' which is the subject of interest. This leads to those problems previously discussed in relation to the fictitious animation of the inanimate: the passivity of the audience, and the need to insist on a plurality of functions within one illustration. As must be clear by now, the indeterminacy of picture perception is in the beholder, not in the picture itself, but the assumption that the picture is active entails the suggestion that some modification of the *picture* is necessary in order to change the perception of that picture. This tends to obscure or eliminate the possibility that there may be nothing 'wrong' with a particular illustration but the audience may not know how to use it. The consequence of this possibility in terms of teaching is significant. It may well be necessary as a preliminary to the effective use of illustrations to provide students with skills in their use — this point will be developed further. The second qualification that needs to be made about this kind of content analysis is that it contains inherent weaknesses which are common to all forms of content analysis. They start by presuming the integrity of the message, but this leads to a contradiction. It is impossible on the basis of a content analysis to infer reliably the intentions of authors or the reactions of audiences, but paradoxically it is impossible to undertake any kind of content analysis without making some kinds of inference about authors or audiences. A further weakness which stems from the peculiarly tenuous and ambiguous relation between message, author and audience in content analysis is that it is impossible to challenge a particular content analysis by using a different content analysis of the same material. The difficulty, which is logical rather than empirical, is that it is impossible to defend any particular content analysis from attack by a rival analysis because in order to conduct the analysis in the first place it is necessary to presume that the meaning of messages is commonly agreed.. This can never be tested by a refinement of content analysis. Content analysis is at best a useful hypothesis but it needs more than an alternative analysis. None the less the merits of the exercise as a preliminary to more soundly based research should not be underrated.

It is however necessary to try to locate the analysis more accurately. Is it a study of Open University texts in relation to their user audience or is it a study of the texts in relation to their authors? Because the study was conducted from within the Open University, it seems reasonable to view it as an analysis of the author/message relation. The learner is therefore a construction — as much part of the analysis as the evolved classification system. The analysis is an investigation into the purposes for which illustrations were intended by authors and designers of Open University texts, and involves the construction of an ideal student — a hypothetical entity who will use the illustrations in a manner consistent with authors' intentions. Such a fiction is a useful starting point in exploring the potential and real relations between learners and illustrations.

In their summary, the authors discovered the following kinds of explicative illustrations: Descriptive, Expressive, Constructional, Functional, Logico-mathematical, Algorithmic and Data display. In this chapter I will examine the first four in detail and turn to the remaining three in the next chapter.

Descriptive Illustrations

Duchastel and Waller define this function as being 'to show what an object looks like'. This is neither as simple as it may seem nor as straightforward as they suggest. Honore Daumier, the nineteenth-century artist, is reputed to have said that photographs described everything and explained nothing (Szarkowski, 1973, p. 72). By way of counter Szarkowski suggested that it could be said of some highly mannered painting that it explained everything and described nothing. It is doubtful whether any of the photographers quoted in the last chapter would have accepted Daumier's verdict but the suggested polarity is worth bearing in mind when examining the ways in which illustrations can be used.

Let us begin with an obvious basis of comparison between photographs and the hand-made image: the draughtsman's range of choices in terms of subject matter are available to any photographer, but the photographer is limited to the consequences of light. The draughtsman by contrast is limited only by hand, eye and imagination — far more flexible tools but ones which require the draughtsman to abstract rather than record. The multiformity of shape, texture, colour and tone present in the environment cannot be fully matched by any artists' palette, however skilfully deployed, which means that artists cannot reproduce nature; they must select those features that are important to them. A tree may have many thousands of leaves, branches, twigs and markings on the bark. No artist would attempt to copy such detail in its entirety; for one thing the picture would be on a much smaller scale so a great deal of detail would be lost, but, more important, it would not seem necessary to reproduce such a degree of detail of an individual specimen. And therein lies the clue as to what guides the choices made by an artist. What is abstracted as significant is dependent on the purpose for which the picture is made, the schemata of the artist and the skills available to him or her. The history of art in relation to these processes of abstraction is eloquently described by Gombrich (1960).

When we say of a picture, then, that it shows what an object looks like, we are saying something quite complex. We do not mean that it is indistinguishable from the object it looks like. We mean that in some important or significant way the picture has properties that make it possible for us to relate it to that object.

It is in the elaboration of the relations between pictures and their subject that the simplistic notion of 'looks like' becomes strained and distended to the point where it is no longer of value and the terms 'description' and 'explanation' become more useful.

We can get some sense of what is involved by using a convenient historical example. Ivins, in his account of the development of prints in visual communication, shows how the conception of botanic illustration changed significantly over a very brief historical period

(Ivins, 1953). Until the advent of printing processes the science of botany was severely hampered; without accurately repeatable visual statements, i.e. prints, the science could not progress.

The Greek botanists realised the necessity of visual statements to give their verbal statements intelligibility. They tried to use pictures for the purpose, but their only ways of making pictures were such that they were utterly unable to repeat their visual statements wholly and exactly. The result was such a distortion at the hands of the successive copyists that the copies became not a help but an obstacle to the clarification and the making precise of their verbal descriptions. And so the Greek botanists gave up trying to use illustrations in their treatises and tried to get along as best they could with words. But, with words alone, they were unable to describe their plants in such a way that they could be recognised — for the same things bore different names in different places. So, finally, the Greek botanists gave up even trying to describe their plants in words, and contented themselves by giving all the names they knew for each plant and then told what human ailments it was good for. In other words, there was a complete breakdown of scientific description and analysis once it was confined to words without demonstrative pictures. (ibid., p. 15)

More recently in an elegant experiment Bartlett showed how, through successive reproduction, an original image becomes degraded and transformed at the hands of successive copyists (Bartlett, 1932) (see Figure 18).

With the invention of printing processes the potential for accurate reproduction was realised, but at first, as Ivins shows, the significance of illustrations was not properly understood, and the woodcuts illustrating herbals were nothing more than decorative motifs only remotely related to the original. They reached their nadir, according to Ivins, in the *Grete Herbal* published in London in 1525 (see Figure 19). A return to direct observation was evident in Brunfel's *Herbarum vivae eicones* published in Augsburg in 1530 (Figure 20). There is no doubting the difference between these two illustrations. Unlike the earlier illustration the latter is the result of careful observation of a particular specimen. Only fifteen years later another change is observable; the 'Kappiskraut' in Fuchs' *De Stirpium Historia*, published in Basle in 1545, is not the result of observing an individual plant but the consequence of observing a number of examples of the

Figure 18: Bartlett's Experiment in Serial Reproduction

Source: Frederic C. Bartlett, *Remembering: A Study in Experimental and Social Psychology* (Cambridge University Press, London, 1932).

Figure 19: Woodcut of a Violet from the *Grete Herbal*

Source: By permission of the Metropolitan Museum of Art.

same plant and drawing their common characteristics (Figure 21).

Now in all these cases we might say that the illustrations are descriptive and provide an account of what the objects look like. But it is quite clear that the term 'looks like' does not allow us to capture the nuances of critical difference which apply to each. In the first the artist is offering a cliche, in the second an individual observation and in the third an abstraction. The relation between the drawings and their subjects, from the point of view of the artists and herbalists, must be seen as descriptions or explanations of and about plants, whereas from the piont of view of the users of such books their adequacy would be entirely a function of the users' expectations. If we wished to use

Figure 20: Woodcut of a Violet from Brunfel's *Herbarum*

Source: By permission of the Metropolitan Museum of Modern Art.

Figure 21: Woodcut of 'Kappiskraut' in Fuch's *De Stirpum Historia*

Braſsicæ quartum genus.
Kappißkraut.

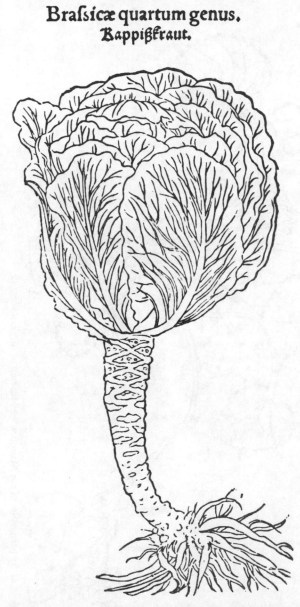

Source: By permission of the Metropolitan Museum of Modern Art.

them as a basis for identifying particular plants, it seems plausible that
the third would be most suitable. Certainly botanists nowadays use
illustrations that follow this principle of abstraction as opposed to any
of the others.

It is worth considering the rationale behind such drawings, and
show parallels with other human activities. The violet in the *Grete
Herbal* is not unlike hearsay: it is at the very least twice removed from
the source of origin and possibly more. It is a rumour — a botanist's
equivalent of gossip; we associate it with a careless disregard of facts
and the imposition of an impoverished and banal point of view. To
make this criticism we must have some notion of what constitutes an
alternative point of view. In this case our observation of actual plants
and other drawings of plants acts as a standard of comparison. It is
only against this later acquired knowledge that any criticism is
possible. Before we condemn the artist and publisher we should
seriously question what standard of evidence, in this or other fields,
was known to the authors. Criticism always requires the pre-existence
of an alternative point of view. This should be borne in mind when
considering the educational uses of illustration. If that use is to be
critical it requires at the very least that the student realises that there
are alternative possibilities and, as I have previously said, one has to
start from the proposition that the subject matter is inherently worthy
of intelligent consideration.

The violet illustration in Brunfel's *Herbarum* is in quite a different
category. It is an eye-witness report. Once again it is against some pre-
existent standard that we judge it. Our criteria would be very like those
we might apply to a newspaper reporter's account. Notions such as
objectivity, impartiality and sensitivity to detail are brought into play.
As must be apparent from much of what has been said so far, the
notion of objectivity might be suspect; ideas informing the artist's
work are not brought into question by the work itself. A reporter does
not cover a story with a view to examining the method of story
coverage. Methods of investigation are in a sense passive tools taken
for granted. The critical activity if any is directed towards the
particular event or object described, the framework for that criticism
is assumed. This is another way of describing the notion of schemata.
In this case the artist is applying a schema — a set of rules the purpose
of which is to provide a framework for sensitive, eye-witness
reportage.

By contrast the illustration in Fuchs' *Herbal* may be seen as careful
observation for the purposes of forming a new schema. It is the

previous example turned inside out. Even the working method of the artist gives a hint to the difference — the drawing is not the result of observing a single plant but the consequence of many observations of varieties of plants. The relationship between drawing and subject is closely akin to the relationship between theory and observation. A theory is a set of generalisations based on multiple observations — or at least it is an attempt to explain a multiplicity of phenomena within a single coherent account. In this case the drawing does not 'look like' any particular specimen. It is a distilled generalisation based on many observations. As such it is a kind of visual theory. This account opens up many avenues of insight. It would suggest that critical judgement of the drawing would, like theory, depend on the available evidence and the ability to match the drawing with that evidence.

Each individual specimen bears the marks of its environmental history but clearly the illustration is devoid of such particularities, which suggests a basic distinction between inherent characteristics and life experience — the basic nature/nurture distinction which is so much a part of biological sciences. In this instance all trace of individuality, of nurture, has been expunged and we are left with an essence — an abstraction — the species. This kind of illustration represents a significant step forward in the science of botany. Comparing it with the earlier Brunfel illustration, which contains the life history of a particular plant, it is obvious that a very different process of abstraction is at work. As the science of botany advanced the basic principle seen at work in the Fuchs' *Herbal* was used to guide the classification of plants. However, there is not a simple dichotomy between the particular and the general. Brunfel's illustration, for all its particularity, is bounded by certain abstractions. The woodcut used in the printing process imposes severe limitations on the quality of line possible, and it completely inhibits the use of tonal gradation and colour. (In later herbals this was sometimes overcome by hand-finishing.) The use of line to delineate contour, shape and volume is in itself a kind of abstraction. It is possible to describe the application of these abstracting principles as the application of a *theory* of representation to a particular object. Art historians often refer to this notion of theory as 'style'. It is an artist's way of coming to terms with experience, which in itself is too rich and varied to represent. It is precisely analogous to scientists' use of theory to grasp the essentials of the phenomena they seek to explain. Thus we can draw many parallels between drawings and theories; we can see both as instruments used to explain and describe.

Explanation and Description

In order to understand the theoretical status of drawings it is
necessary to look more closely at the terms 'description' and
'explanation', which so far in this text have not been adequately
qualified. To describe something is essentially to transpose it, that is,
one takes an object, event or process, and using words, pictures or
some other symbolic system one gives an account of it. It is a kind of
translation from one form to another. In description there is an
assumption that the phenomenon being described is intrinsically
intelligible, and the act of description is simply a temporal or spatial
transfer. For example, a radio commentator at a football match is
observing something that we assume to be intrinsically intelligible; his
description of that match to the listeners is essentially a spatial
transposition — the football match is in a sense moved from the
playing field into the listeners' living rooms. A drawing can be used in
exactly this way. It offers an account, a description, of something
which is not immediately present.

There is an interesting and often complex relation between the
form and content of descriptions. This is readily apparent in simple
cases such as the woodcut used in herbals, but there are areas of much
greater importance and intricacy. The description of the war in
Vietnam used a variety of forms: most notably, the photographic and
film coverage of that war has been pointed to as an important
contributing factor in shaping public opinion.

Before considering this kind of complex relation it is necessary to
examine the term 'explanation'. Whereas a description of something
assumes it to be intelligible, an explanation assumes that in some
respect the phenomenon is unintelligible and the act of explanation is
a process of making it intelligible. Thus whereas a description
transposes a phenomenon, an explanation transforms it and it does so
in the direction of greater intelligibility (at least that is the assumption
guiding the act of explanation).

We can usefully recast these actions of description and explanation
into our framework of author/message and audience/message relations. An author involved in a process of description must assume two
things about the audience: first, that the audience, if present, would
perceive in a like manner the phenomenon being described, and
secondly, that the form (or symbolic system) used in the description is
commonly understood by both author and audience. By contrast the
author involved in explanation, while believing that he shares with the

audience an understanding of the form being used, assumes that the phenomenon being explained is *not* intelligible to the audience and that the explanation offered will make it so. Thus the author is operating from a position of declared privilege. Describing is like opening a door; explaining is like opening a locked door.

However, there is a point at which the differences between explanation and description merge and the distinction between the two is false. That point is reached when the focus is shifted away from the phenomena and on to the form. No symbolic system is neutral with respect to its subject matter. A language, a picturing style, a mathematical system, imposes limitations and selections on the data available. What may be thought of as an act of transposition is always an act of transformation.

When we come to examine the audience/message relation with respect to any particular description or explanation we will see the full extent of the overlapping and interpenetration of these two modes. Presented with pictures like those in the herbals most of us, I suspect, would be inclined to say that they offer us descriptions rather than explanations about plants. In doing so we are making two assumptions. First, we are constructing an author with a particular intent, which leads us to a critical comparison of the abilities of the different artists to fulfil that intent. It is against some ideal that we make that judgement. Secondly, there must be a belief in the integrity and honesty of the author for us to accept the description. Our primary interest is in the content itself — the plant or whatever else is described.

However, suppose, for whatever reason, we believed that the account given does not accord with our perceptions of related phenomena; that, say, the violet in the *Grete Herbal*, even if we had never seen a real violet, is of dubious quality as a description. Two things happen: we begin to question the integrity of the artist, and we become acutely critical of the form of representation. In other words we become aware that a transformation (albeit a very crude and impoverishing one) has been applied. We may see the same principle at work in the contemporary critique of advertising. Starting from the belief that the account of the world shown in advertising does not accord with our perception of the world as we find it in our daily lives, the analysis seeks to expose the transformation which advertisers apply to our world when they create advertisements. Most of the work in this area is speculative — the analyses are not of actual transformations but of inferred transformations based on an analysis of advertisements; but they attempt to show that what may be offered in advertisements as descriptions can very interestingly be understood as explanations — a justification of a false set of ideas. Similarly, the suppression of authorship we have previously noted in photography works in the reverse direction moving an explanation into a description. Without an author a photograph is simply a transposition of the world 'as is'. Equally, there are many instances where an explanation becomes so widely accepted that the transformations associated with it sink below the surface and simply become redundant. Concepts like 'gravity' or 'electron', which are part of the explanatory systems of particular theories in physics, have become so widely known that we associate them directly with particular phenomena rather than with the explanations for phenomena. What was originally a brilliant transformation appears to us a simple transposition, that is, it has become a name for something which is believed to exist rather than a theoretical construct within an explanation. Central to this summary, and what makes the contast between description and explanation so important in this context, is the proposition that description and explanation are ways of relating to messages and as such may differ within our two units of analysis. Thus what may be offered by an author as a description can be perceived as an explanation by an audience and vice versa.

We now return to the more specific use of drawings and examine their theoretical status. There can be no doubt that a drawing could be used by students in either a descriptive or explanatory relation. However, there is a need to specify the conditions which would precipitate either use of illustrations. As will be clear from earlier chapters, I am of the opinion that the dominant expectation of pictures is that they are to be used as simple descriptions. This is clear from psychological and pedagogic literature. Their use as explanations would seem by comparison to be largely underdeveloped and certainly unexplored outside certain narrow areas of specialism. Thus the question of their theoretical status hardly arises. There are two strands to this which interact. The first, already discussed, is the relegation of pictorial material to a category of unimportant media — by comparison with the written word and numbers, pictures are not important. The second strand (and in part related to the first) is that pictures are considered unproblematic. This has had the widespread effect of leading educational technologists to believe that using pictures is synonymous with making things simpler, more comprehensible.

I suspect that we might well be approaching a general crisis in this area — if we are not already in its midst. This simple faith in pictures seems to be losing adherents, and we may find in that some hope and a direction for a healthier use of pictures in future. We need a crisis in confidence. We need a sceptical framework from which to challenge the belief in the unproblematic nature of drawings. It is easy when confronted with the *Grete Herbal* to doubt the status of the illustration but it becomes much harder to challenge it in the later works. Our scepticism, so well honed to the printed word, is a blunt instrument when applied to drawings, but in principle the task is similar. It requires skill, which is obtained through repeated practice and encouragement; and it requires an anti-authoritarian view of knowledge — the right of any individual to question the legitimacy or truthfulness of authoritative knowledge and opinion. How many of us would doubt, outside the context of this book, the truthfulness or correctness of the illustrations from the later herbals? It is only when confronted with a blatant travesty that our credulity is strained. Much that is a commonly accepted element of intellectual life when dealing with language fails us with the drawn image; we need to consider the development of illustrations as explanatory systems within a much wider critical framework, at present lying beyond the immediate horizon.

In the best traditions of intellectual scepticism we need to question the truthfulness of illustrations. Once we do so we not only discover their weaknesses but the act of questioning transforms them from descriptions to explanations. It is clear that to develop this intellectual explanation requires more than careful attention to illustrations. It also requires that students develop a certain style of reading. I suggested in the last chapter that our central question in relation to the use of illustrations in texts should be concerned with the schemata students deploy in using them. How can these be developed? In this chapter I have borrowed a visual argument from Ivins. The juxtaposition of three illustrations has enabled us to explore some very important avenues and we have by no means exhausted the possibilities — we have merely scratched the surface. Contrasting this approach with the normal use of illustrations there is one stark difference. Normally one would find in a book only one illustration used for a particular purpose. By contrast, if a controversial subject is being dealt with, it is usual to find in the written part of the text, a selection of arguments for or against a particular view and sometimes a possibility of multiple view points (the very phrase 'view points' hints at what is offered). How often is there an equivalent controversy in illustrations? The singularity of illustrations makes them authoritative, beyond criticism. 'Here is a picture of a nuclear power station; here is the controversy (in words) surrounding it.' What, and in whose mind, would constitute a simple descriptive illustration of a nuclear power station? However, it is not sufficient simply to thrust a new mode of usage on to the unsuspecting student. Any text which adopts the strategy outlined above must present students with guidelines on why it is being done and what is expected. There is an unfortunate tendency among educators, which I have already noted, to treat visual aids as if they were a kind of intravenously administered knowledge, their potency deriving from their ability to drip past the critical faculties directly into the mind. My view on this matter is clear. If they drip past our critical faculties they drip out, not in. If illustrations are to be used well we must educate the users to appreciate their importance.

Expressive Illustrations

Continuing with the use of Duchastel and Waller's classification, their account of the function of expressive illustrations is: 'To make an impact on the reader beyond simple description . . . Pictures of war or famine victims add to the credibility of a purely verbal message' (1979, pp. 21 and 24).

Notice how clearly the epistemological status of the illustration is revealed. A photograph is assumed to lend credibility. This is a clear demonstration of the authoritative status accorded to illustrations. While acknowledging that photographs are frequently used in this way, particularly in newspapers, it seems to me a use which is inconsistent with a sceptical framework. It belongs more within a rhetorical context. I am not suggesting that students should not be exposed to persuasive or partisan material; a great deal of education would simply be operating under false pretenses if it claimed to be otherwise. But whereas the mechanisms of verbal rhetoric are widely understood, visual rhetoric is not so easily accessible. It exists none the less and is regularly used even in education. Gaining access to it, so that we can better understand the forms it takes, has proved enormously difficult. Part of the problem has been a lack of conceptual clarity. Many studies have been motivated by politically radical perspectives which have made very wide assumptions about the effects of rhetoric, but one of the most serious obstacles in the way of studying visual rhetoric is the lack of an adequate methodology. One of the earliest and to my mind still one of the most important contributions in the field comes from the Ulm School of Design (Bonsiepe, 1961). By using the terminology and classifications derived from studies of verbal rhetoric an attempt was made to describe the structural differences of advertising messages. There are many problems, as can be seen from a careful scrutiny of this study, but questions are raised which challenge any assertion that the relation between pictures and their meaning is simple. The definition given by Duchastel and Waller contains the idea that 'expressive illustrations' go 'beyond simple description'. We have seen in the previous section how complex a 'simple description' can be! In this section I want to explain some aspects of illustration that go a long way beyond the point reached so far.

Rhetoric has frequently been maligned as the province of salesmen and politicians. A language free of such devices has been the ambition of many logicians and scientists but this has obscured the very frequent and important use of rhetorical devices in their own exacting subjects amongst others. At the basis of verbal rhetoric is the use of non-literal language — what we commonly refer to as figures of speech. Metaphor, simile, metonymy, zeugma and synecdoche are a few examples. The essence of the Ulm enquiry was to explore how far these classifications in verbal rhetoric could be matched to figurative uses of visual material.

As an example, and using material that it would be difficult to argue as fitting into conventional notions of persuasive material, I have chosen some commonly used information symbols (Figure 22). Throughout this brief analysis I shall be concerned with the author/ message relation. Whether these symbols are widely understood or not, though in the long term more important, will not be considered at this stage. I shall be concerned purely with the relations between these symbols and what they are intended to represent.

The first symbol, 'airport', is a visual example of synecdoche — the relation between the symbol and what it stands for is a relation of part to whole. The aircraft is only a part of what we would find at an airport. In order to move from the symbol 'aircraft' to airport requires a particular kind of transformation, which, if spelled out, is 'If you go to this place you will find facilities related to the use of this object'. The second symbol, 'scenic lookout', obviously requires a very different transformation. Here the normal range of verbal figurative

Figure 22: Some Commonly Used Information Symbols

devices deserts us; in effect the relation, if spelled out, is: 'This is an appropriate place to use this object'. In the final symbol, 'fragile', we find yet another transformation employed. It is not unlike a simile. Hence the relation, if we spell it out, is 'If you do not handle these goods with care, what has happened to this glass could happen to them'. The simile comes in the idea that the objects on which the symbol is found have similar properties to glass, but there is a further element that we might describe as narrative consequential: 'if this is done, that will follow'. Once again we have a very different transformation from the first two. My point in offering this analysis is not to suggest that it is the only, or necessarily the best, way to describe the transformations used in the design of these symbols but to open up for scrutiny a very complex area of investigation that must form part of any account of visual communication.

Returning to the notion of 'expressive' illustrations we can now get a slightly clearer sense of what is involved. The picture of the famine victim or the battle scene is not used to provide information about that victim or that battle scene in the way the botanic illustration provides information about that plant. Their use is more akin to that of the aircraft in relation to the airport. It is a part standing for the whole or perhaps the particular standing for the general. This in itself raises questions of typicality. We have got used to the 'look' of war or famine in photographs. How far does that expectation inform the press photographer or the newspaper editor when they make selections on our behalf? Those are questions that must form part of any use made of illustrations in this non-literal context.

However if we move our considerations into the audience/message relation we are confronted by another set of problems. Does the audience have the necessary cognitive skills to effect the required transformations? In the area of public information symbols, for which some data is available (Cairney and Sless, 1980), it is clear that users make very few errors at the level of transposition, that is, recognising aircraft, cameras and glasses. Where the majority of errors do occur is in the transformations applied to the symbols. This suggests an important area of learning which is presently unexplored and it further suggests that changing the symbols may not improve user comprehension, as users will still apply incorrect transformations. If we transfer that conclusion to the educational uses of illustration then we are once more confronted with the need to focus attention onto the students and the skills they have for transforming visual material.

Finally in exploring figurative aspects of illustrations we need to consider one of the supreme achievements of human intellect: the development of scientific theories. It is seldom acknowledged that visual thinking and in particular the exploitation of visual metaphors have played a very important role in the generation of theory.

Many of our most important theories owe their origins in part to visual thinking. The Ptolemaic system and the Copernican system which followed it both relied on a visual model and this in turn was developed to provide models of the behaviour of gases and early models of atomic structure.

Einstein described his thinking as follows:

The words of the language, as they are spoken or written, do not seem to play any role in my mechanism of thought. The psychical entities which seem to serve as elements in thought are certain signs and more or less clear images which can be voluntarily reproduced and combined . . . The above-mentioned elements are in my case of visual and some muscular type. Conventional words or other signs have to be sought for laboriously in a secondary stage, when the above-mentioned associative play is sufficiently established and can be reproduced at will. (Einstein quoted in Hadamard, 1945, pp. 142-3)

Kekulé's account of his discovery of the benzine ring in a dream is instructive:

Again the atoms were gamboling before my eyes. Smaller groups kept to the background. My mind's eye trained by repeated visions of a similar kind, now distinguished larger formations of various shapes . . . everything in movement winding and turning like snakes. And look, what was that? One snake grabbed its own tail, and mockingly the shape whirled before my eyes. As if struck by lightning I awoke. (Anschutz, 1961)

Kekulé realised that organic molecules like benzine are not open structures but closed rings. It is interesting that at school Kekulé excelled in mathematics and *drawing*.

Finally Watson's account of the discovery of DNA provides us with further evidence of visual thinking in science.

Only a little encouragement was needed to get the final soldering accomplished in the next couple of hours. The brightly shining metal plates were then immediately used to make a model in which for the first time all the DNA components were present. In about an hour I had arranged the atoms in positions which satisfied both the X-ray data and the laws of stereochemistry. The resulting helix was righthanded with the two chains running in opposite directions. (Watson, 1968)

All of these accounts testify to the existence of a powerful intellectual tool; a skill which has to be learnt to be effectively used.

Here is one area of education complementary to our present discussion that has often received attention under the heading of creativity. Many of the visual transformations to be found in visual communication have been systematically explored in the pioneer work of synectics (Gordon, 1961), and popularised by de Bono. Whatever may be claimed as the value of such techniques it is significant to see them as closely related to the transformations we have explored in this chapter. It may well be that the underlying cognitive processes have much in common.

Constructional Illustrations

As I sit at my desk, I am surrounded on all sides by objects that are the end-product of a process of manufacture. It is reasonably certain that at some stage in that process the form of the object will have been drawn so as to communicate to someone how it was to be made, assembled or maintained. Technical drawings form an integral and necessary part of industrial society. Without the conventions and skills of the draughtsman the complex machinery that forms part of our society simply could not exist. It is this important use of drawings which Duchastel and Waller refer to as 'constructional'. A recent exhibition organised by the Welsh Arts Council (Welsh Arts Council, 1978) celebrated the wealth of engineering drawing produced over the last 200 years. In an essay in the catalogue, Ken Baynes and Francis Pugh make some useful functional distinctions which provide a fascinating insight into the relation between different kinds of drawing and the production process. Briefly these are:

1. Designers' Drawings: these are preliminary sketches which provide basic working ideas, usually no more than rough sketches (Figure 23).
2. Project Drawings: generalised as in the previous category but usually produced in a more formal style. Their purpose in relation to the process of production is to provide an informed audience with a general outline of a proposal (Figure 24).
3. Production Drawings: these form an integral part of the production process. It is the information in these that leads directly to the fabrication of parts on the factory floor. As such they can actually be seen as a key link in the control of production (Figure 25).
4. Presentation or Maintenance Drawings: produced after the product is completed as a guide to routine maintenance or alternatively as a celebration of the product for marketing purposes (Figure 26).
5. Technical Illustration: it is this latter category which one thinks of most typically as part of the pedagogic process, explaining how things work (Figure 27).

My summary cannot possibly do justice to the kind of drawing about which it can be said, as of no other, that it shaped the lives of the vast majority of the population in industrial society over the last 200 years. As Christopher Jones suggests (Jones, 1970), the transition from craft-based to manufacturing industry was also a transition in

Figure 23: A Sketch by Sir Herbert Austin

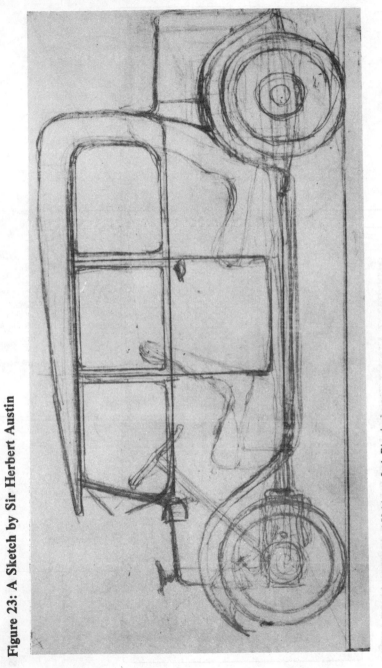

Source: Leyland Historical Vehicles, Ltd, Birmingham.

Figure 24: A Weight Diagram for a Projected 2.4.42T Locomotive

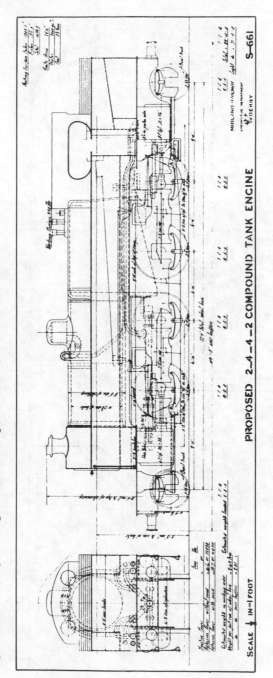

Source: The National Railway Museum, York.

Figure 25: A Drawing Showing the Main Landing Gear Assembly for the VC 10 Aircraft

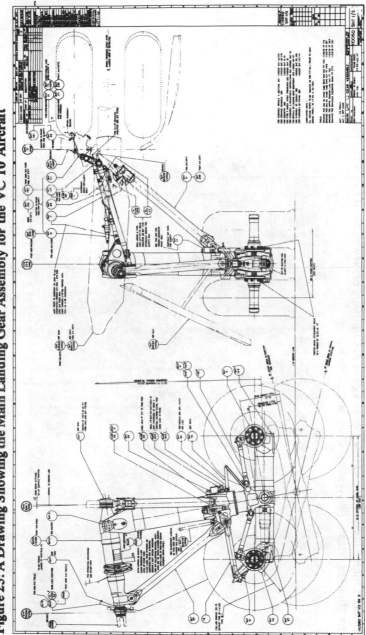

Source: British Aerospace, Weybridge.

Figure 26: An 'As Fitted' Drawing of a Pair of Ships, the Grand Duke Constantine and Grand Duke Alexis built by Hawthorne Leslie & Company of Newcastle-upon-Tyne for the Russian Steam Navigation Company, 1890.

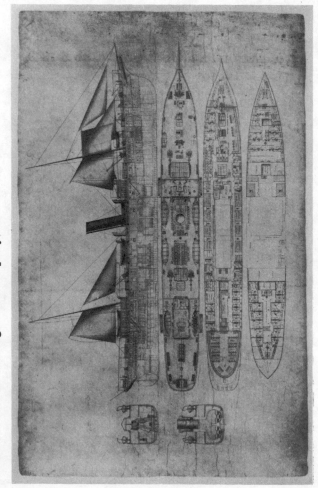

Figure 27: A Lubrication Diagram Issued by the Air Ministry Directorate of Technical Development, 1930.

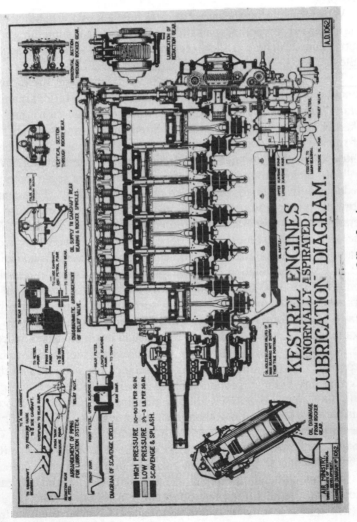

Source: The Controller of Her Majesty's Stationery Office, London.

design methods. Using drawings instead of memorised routines the 'perceptual span' of the designer increased. Visual thinking was separated from the making of objects and took place on paper. This led to specifying the form of things in advance of manufacture which in turn enabled the process of manufacture to be broken down into different parts. The division of labour closely parallels the growth of engineering drawing. However, the increased perceptual span also meant that design and hence manufacture could be much more complex.

When considering the larger role of visual education in our society, the increased perceptual span afforded by drawing is something which curriculum designers in all subjects would do well to take into account (Sless, 1978).

The above classification of engineering drawings in terms of function is based on a contemporary analysis of historical material. Many drawings were used for a variety of functions and the classification reflects the increased differentiation and specialisation of roles within industrial society. It is possible that with increased automation and computer-aided design some of these categories may collapse into each other or disappear, but there are some important pedagogic insights to be derived from this history. Engineering drawing is a paradigm case of visual communication where the relation of author/message and audience/message is constantly put to the test of effectiveness. This depends on a common purpose of manufacture, a shared body of knowledge and conventions and above all an economic relation of ownership and production. In a general sense the workers' job depends on the accurate understanding of the drawing. These imperatives do not surround the understanding of many of the forms of visual communication that we have so far examined; but, in all those areas where such imperatives do operate, i.e. where the reading of a drawing forms part of a determined economic relation, that drawing is subject to a rigorous set of conventions both of production and reading. Moreover, it exists within a framework where only one meaning is expected. Curiously this can be transformed by changing the framework. The drawings in the above exhibition, removed from workshops, factories and drawing boards, take on a formal elegance through the eyes of anyone sensitive to formalist aesthetics. They can also take on a metonymic function in relation to such concepts as work, factory, industry, mass production or the golden age of steam. However, in their original context it was clear that only one meaning was to be derived from their reading, which contrasts sharply with many other forms of communication where no such imperative operates, or at best operates only weakly. This contrast is between a monosemic (single meaning) context and a polysemic (many meaning) context. Note that it is not the message itself which determines which category it will occupy but the context in which it is used. Educationalists desiring to maximise effectiveness, while ignoring such contextual determinants, have not learnt a very basic lesson.

Functional Illustration

The final category in this chapter is something of a hybrid. Duchastel and Waller define it as 'enabling the learner to visually follow through the unfolding of a process or the organisation of a system' (see Figure 28). A defining characteristic of this kind of illustration is that it involves a transformation from non-visible processes to the visible representations in the author/message relation and vice versa in the audience/message relation. It is assumed that some aspect of the phenomenon is not apprehendable directly. Some temporal or spatial continuity which is not immediately apparent is presented to link entities which are visible. More than any other kind of drawing this shows the close link between visual processes and the activity of theory construction. But it crosses the boundary between drawings and diagrams which are the central concern of the next chapter. There are issues concerned with the comprehensibility of such drawings which cannot be answered by reference to a specific set of conventions, because there tends, in this form, to be an *ad hoc* relation between a variety of different conventions which may or may not generate ambiguities in the reading. I have already established the basic principles of analysis which apply to such material; two points, however, are worth raising. First, the mixing of different modes of representation in one illustration might from a purist point of view be considered undesirable. (I know of no evidence either for or against such a view but it seems worthy of further investigation.) Secondly, in illustrations of this kind spatial configuration plays a key role. The Gestalt laws mentioned in Chapter 3, which, despite their limited significance, played such a large part in twentieth-century design aesthetics, do point to a general tendency to organise information in space. How far this tendency controls both the production and reading of such illustrations remains an open question worthy of further investigation. An example of both these issues working (possibly at their worst) can be seen in the Arecibo message.

Figure 28: Functional Illustration

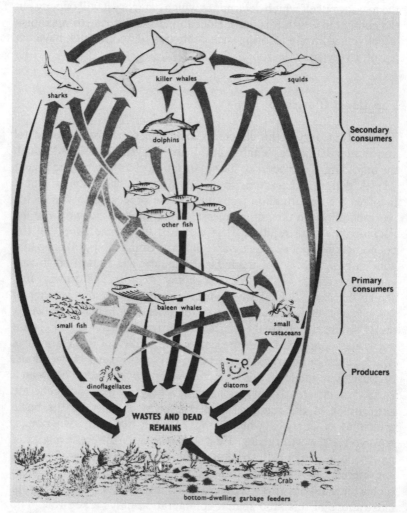

Source: *Biological Science: the Web of Life* (Australian Academy of Science, 1977).

There can be little doubt that illustrations do play an extraordinarily important part in our culture. The dominance of literacy and numeracy in the education system has obscured the central role of these forms in the development of science and engineering which are the backbone of our culture. They are not just aids to learning, playing a peripheral role, but are central to our processes of accumulating knowledge, formulating theory, constructing and controlling our environment. They are the product of centuries of accumulated skill and intellection. The casual approach often adopted by editors and publishers to the use of illustrations in comparison with the dedication and seriousness reserved for written text is only part of the problem; the student in turn must be guided towards a more serious use of visual material before its potential can be realised.

8 GRAPHS AND DIAGRAMS

Introduction

With much of the material I have considered so far the emphasis has been on the variety of possibilities set against a background of a poverty of actual uses; in many instances I have emphasised the polysemic nature of the context against the monosemic nature of intentions. In this chapter the focus will be on material where variety, in part, gives way to precision. Like botanic illustration in a scientific context and engineering drawing in the context of production, many charts and diagrams depend on precision. It is possible to offer at the outset a generalisation about such material: as the uses of such material have become more and more rigorous there has been a tendency to systematise and codify the areas of permissible trans- formation and the rules of presentation; such tendencies can be observed throughout the history of these forms. There is, accordingly, no shortage of texts describing various forms of graphs and diagrams and their application, so this chapter will not be devoted to a repetition of that material.

Despite the existence, in many cases, of clear conventions, there are large areas of choice where it is not immediately obvious which graphic layout is best suited to a particular purpose. Not surprisingly, because of the precision of the information and the apparent exactitude of the tasks associated with them, graphs and diagrams have attracted experimental psychologists — there is an interesting chronicle of research in this field which more so than in any other area of visual communication demonstrates the weaknesses of naive experimentation and the strength of wise practice. Unlike photographs or drawings, where it remains largely the case that generalisation is properly beyond our reach, graphs and diagrams provide an area where some generalisation is possible. I shall try to show that this is less due to underlying psychological constructs and more related to a precise matching of material and task definition. Simply, users can perform tasks, if they know precisely what the task is and the material is designed specifically with that task in mind. What may prove more interesting in the long run, in this particular area of visual communi- cation, is not any supposed psychological constants which entice those who seek unreasonable control over the learning process but the prodigious capacity of diagrams to sustain complex visual thinking.

I will begin by describing the range of material to be considered and then give an account of the peculiar characteristics of visual thought which graphs and diagrams utilise to such advantage. The lessons of research in the field will then be considered and I will end by tempting the reader to consider the exciting potential of these devices in the future of human intellectual activity.

The Range of Material

I shall continue to use Duchastel and Waller's categories as a way of indicating the range of material that will be covered (Duchastel and Waller, 1979). Their next category is what they call 'Logico-mathematical', and it involves the uses of visual means for representing 'mathematical concepts' (ibid., p. 24). The example they give is a line graph (see Figure 29), which is not so much a mathematical concept as a form of data display. Maintaining our functional stance, its use is most likely to be to provide numerical data of trends. In that context it might serve to illustrate the application of a mathematical concept, but in doing so, it functions metonymically.

The category is worth preserving despite the poor example, as it is extremely important. Mathematics and logic are in an important sense visual. Mathematical symbols are the basis of mathematical operations, so the form they take is an integral part of the concepts. This is most obvious in geometry and in graphs but even the solution of equations is in part a visual operation (try solving a quadratic equation using mental arithmetic!). The advent of computers will undoubtedly alter the historical development of mathematical reasoning by allowing operations to be performed electronically but, as we shall see, mathematical reasoning is intimately linked to visual thought.

The second category, 'Algorithmic diagrams' (see Figure 30), form a group which includes ordinary language algorithms, operation research flow charts, and the many derivations of this basic systems-thinking approach.

The final category, 'Data display' (see Figure 31), represents a large category of different devices all of which transform or transpose numerical information into a graphic form.

These three categories represent the range of material which this chapter will handle. The issues I shall deal with are those which are

Figure 29: Line Graph

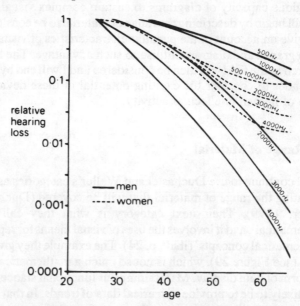

Curves for hearing loss with ageing for men and women. The graph shows the hearing loss expressed in relation to the sensitivity at 25 years to a 4 000 Hz tone. For example, the hearing sensitivity of a 50-year-old man for a tone of 4 000 Hz is about 1/100 of his sensitivity at 25 years.

Source: The Open University.

commonly neglected in the literature on this subject and in keeping with the content of this book I will have more to say about the way we think about them than how we make them.

The Visual Basis

All of the forms discussed in this chapter have something in common. They are techniques for transforming or transposing information from one form which is either impossible or difficult to manipulate or operate upon, into another form which makes those operations possible or easier. They all exploit the human visual system's exceptional capacity for using pattern and all tend to avoid where possible that system's weakness in dealing with quantity.

The invention of graphs can usefully provide us with an example.

Figure 30: Algorithmic Diagram

TRANSPORT FOR THE DISABLED

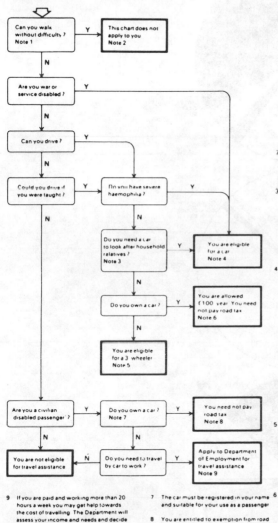

Notes

1   The Act says you are disabled (have difficulty walking) if

 - you have one leg amputated above or through the knee and the other amputated at ove or below the knee
 - you have an organic defect which prevents you from walking (for example a nerve. muscle or bone defect or a severe chronic heart or lung ailment)
 - you can walk only a little and need a vehicle to get to work or to run your household [In this category you will *not* get help if you use a car in the course of your work and you will *not* be helped to get to and from an educational establishment Also the absence or inadequacy of public transport will *not* be taken into account]

2   Other kinds of disability are judged on their merits by the Department of Employment For example, a blind person might receive the taxi fare to and from work

3   You are eligible for a car if

 - you are a disabled parent or guardian in sole charge of young children under 14 for most of the day
 - you are one of two relatives in a house and the other person is blind or disabled This will hold even if the other person is too young or disabled to drive

4   • you will also get free insurance for one driver free road tax and car maintenance at £35 p a for first two years. £55 p a for next two years and £65 p a thereafter (new car) or £40 p a for first two years £65 p a thereafter (reconditioned car)

 - the car must be used only by you or for your purposes
 - the car can be converted to hand control and will eventually be replaced free of charge
 - you may choose an invalid tricycle instead of a car
 - you are *still* eligible even if you already have one or more cars The above four points still apply and if you choose not to have the extra vehicle you may still get the financial support for one car

5   • your 3-wheeler will be a single-seat invalid tricycle

 - it will be driven by petrol or electricity
 - it will be maintained free of charge
 - you will get free third-party insurance and free road tax
 - you must be over 16 to drive this vehicle

6   • the car must be registered and insured in your name

 - you must hold a full driving licence
 - your exemption from road tax only applies as long as the car is used by you or for your purposes

9   If you are paid and working more than 20 hours a week you may get help towards the cost of travelling The Department will assess your income and needs and decide accordingly. You will be reassessed periodically

7   The car must be registered in your name and suitable for your use as a passenger

8   You are entitled to exemption from road tax so long as the vehicle is being used by you or for your purposes

Source: The Open Univesity.

Though earlier attempts are known, the formal basis for our present system dates from 1637 when René Descartes published the book

Figure 31: Data Display

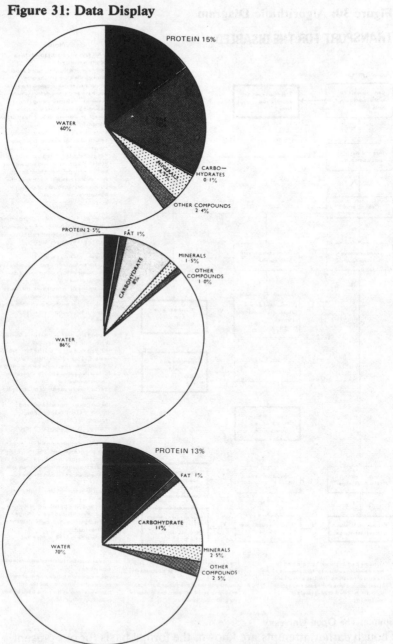

Source: *Biological Science: the Web of Life* (Australian Academy of Science, 1977).

which earned him the title of father of modern philosophy. In an appendix to that work he laid the foundation for a revolution in visual thinking — he invented the graph by combining geometry and algebra. The formal mathematics he accomplished is less significant than his discovery of the power of visual thought. By transforming numerical relations into patterns it is possible to deal with a much wider and more complex mix of data than was previously possible.

Descartes, so the story goes, made this discovery in the time-honoured posture adopted by great thinkers at the moment of insight — on his back (Asimov, 1975). He was, we are told, in bed watching a fly hovering, and wondering how to describe in mathematical terms its position at any moment in time, when it occurred to him that three lines at right angles to each other, intersecting at the location of the fly, would accurately fix its position. Moreover, if the system of notation used to describe this was standardised, three numbers would be sufficient to locate any point in space with respect to a predetermined starting point, or two numbers if the point was on a flat plane. We call the system he devised by various names: Cartesian geometry, after Descartes' Latin name, analytic geometry because algebra used to be called analysis, or co-ordinate geometry after the conventions of co-ordinates which he formulated. It was this invention which provided the basis of the calculus for Newton's physics and gave us a system of visual communication without which modern science would be unthinkable.

Basically what a graph does is present information which is intelligible — more so than it would be if presented by any other known communication system. The reasons for this are not in the mathematics of graphs but in the instrument which interprets them — the human eye — which has a limited capacity to deal with quantity but a remarkable capacity to deal with pattern. This may not seem obvious at first so I will digress from our main interest and look at how we process visual information and in particular our differing capacity for handling quantitative versus qualitative information. How many different typefaces or handwriting can you read? The possibilities are almost infinitely varied. The eye is a superb pattern recognition system, so much so that the limits of its capacity have never been measured nor for that matter is there an adequate theoretical explanation of how the system might work. None of this became apparent until computer programmers tried to program machines to do what the eye does easily — namely read written text. This has proved enormously difficult. Despite all the electronic wizardry the machine remains incapable of duplicating the versatility of human pattern recognition.

But in one important respect the machine has been discovered superior to human vision. It can count and make quantitative judgements with much greater accuracy and speed than the eye. It would take a long time to count the number of cells on a microscope slide by eye, for example. There are machines that can make the count in a fraction of a second. However, where the machine makes mistakes is in identifying what is and what is not a cell. You might like to try a little experiment. Stand well back from a brick wall and try counting the number of bricks. You will find it very difficult to do so. One of the ways we deal with our visual inadequacy with counting is to form patterns, as for example on dominoes and cards, and even in our use of arabic numerals. Each of these has a distinctive pattern which in itself stands for a particular number, thus avoiding the need to count which is stil partially necessary with Roman numerals.

Our limited capacity to count resulted in one of the most important inventions, and one which is seldom acknowledged: the humble ruler. The wheel is often cited as the most important invention in our mastery over our environment. However, without the ruler, the wheel would not have taken us very far. No other single instrument, apart from the hand, occupies such a central role in the process of making. It does what no human eye can do on its own and that is accurately delineate length. It must rank as one of the first visual aids.

It is this transformation into pattern that lies at the heart of all logico-mathematical, algorithmic and data display systems. Our sense of pattern is an extremely important part of all intellectual activity and the externalisation and representation of pattern in visual communication is, as we have repeatedly observed, at the core of many advances.

Some Areas of Doubt and Research

The operation of a system of conventions ensures that choices of alternative methods of representation are determined by rules; provided that both the author and the audience share the same set of rules, communication between the two is by definition effective. The author can foresee and describe accurately the audience/message relation. But any system of rules has limitations, areas of ambiguity, contingencies not covered; or the system may be in a process of change or development and new rules have not been formalised. In short there are, even within the most precise fields of graphic communication, areas of doubt. I have already given a simple example (Figure 14, Chapter 5), but it is remarkable how wide those areas of doubt can be. Two kinds of activity have been used to resolve uncertainties: the accumulated wisdom and knowledge of practitioners, and the evidence from experimental studies. Both of these have been ably reviewed by Michael Macdonald-Ross (Macdonald-Ross, 1977). His approach marks an important new trend in the analysis of visual communication, taking account of many of the criticisms of the educational media research that are made throughout this book; anyone working in this field should pay careful attention both to the underlying concepts and the findings of his review in this area. His conclusions are:

> In general, the advice given by the best practical communicators has been substantially vindicated. One or two research workers quite openly suggested that such advice was just 'a matter of opinion' and hence as likely to be wrong as right. The body of research reviewed here does not bear out this view. On the contrary: there is no known case where a well articulated and deeply held practical viewpoint has been overturned, and many cases where the practitioner has been upheld.

and

> No one graphic format is universally superior to all others, though some are so unsatisfactory that they can be virtually discarded from the armoury. To choose the best format for a particular occasion one must decide: what kind of data is to be shown? What teaching point needs to be made? What will the learner do with the data? Can previous models be copied? Do we have the time and skills to execute the format . . . It pays to remember that graphic communication is an *art*, that is, a skill which results from knowledge and practice. (ibid., pp. 400-1)

As Macdonald-Ross repeatedly demonstrates, even experienced and distinguished researcers such as M.D. Vernon underestimate the importance of the quality of the stimulus material. This is not due to lack of skill on the part of researchers but more to the research tradition in experimental psychology which, as we have seen frequently throughout this text, has failed the researchers because of its conceptual poverty and naive positivism.

Many of the points made in Macdonald-Ross's review are specific to particular graphic forms and will not be reproduced here in this general review; but it is worth examining at least one particular finding in order to show both the strengths of the present state of the art and the weaknesses which persist in the way we handle uncertainties about choices of graphic form.

Graphic experts (such as Brinton, 1916; Karsten, 1923; Neurath, 1936) have advised that the use of circles for showing quantitative data is inferior to bar charts (see Figure 32). It is argued that judgements of length are easier to make than judgements of area or volume. This practical wisdom was challenged by experimental psychologists who were inclined to regard such claims as 'purely matters of opinion' of which 'none show any evidence of an experimental basis of fact' (Eells, 1926). Nothing shows more clearly the contempt of experimental psychology for anything other than knowledge gained by experimental methods. The consequence of this narrow-mindedness has been a long series of experiments, some of which have been wasted because the experimenters failed to understand the nature either of the task or of the stimulus material. Eells (followed and imitated by many of the later researchers) compared segmented bar charts with pie charts (see Figure 33), without noticing that comparing one part of a circle segment with another is essentially either a linear task (comparing relative lengths of circumference), or a matching task (judging how many times a segment will fit into the remaining circle), neither of which demand two- or three-dimensional quantitative skills which are necessary for making relative judgements about circle size, towards which the original advice was directed.

Eventually the experimental research confirmed the practical research of the experts but this left unanswered the problem generated by the use of circles. Human judgement of circle sizes is not only poor but seems to show no consistent pattern of error, or at least the most recent experimental research (Meihoefer, 1969, 1973) casts some doubt on earlier work which suggested that errors followed a consistent pattern. It is only when the procedures for these experiments are examined in detail that it becomes apparent that the problems which bedevilled the earlier research still persist.

First (consistently with much of this type of research), 'The purpose of the tests was not disclosed, in order to minimise bias in the answers' (Meihoefer, 1969, p. 112). Instead subjects were told: 'The

Figure 32: Bar Charts and Circles

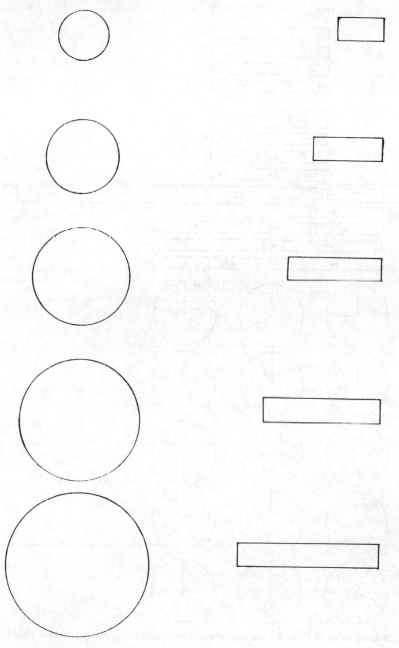

Figure 33: Eells' Experimental Material

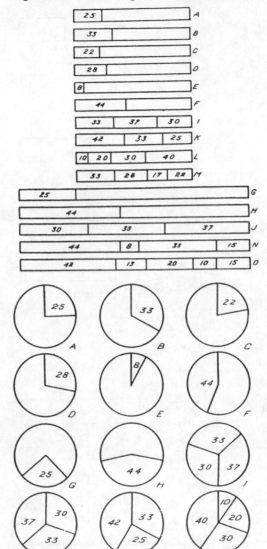

map in front of you is designed to test your reaction to map symbols' (Meihoefer, 1973, p. 67). This is a recurrence of what we observed in Chapter 5. Minimising bias in this case involves systematically misleading subjects about the purpose of the task they are performing! A very different, but I suspect more useful introduction to subjects would have been 'We are investigating how accurately map symbols convey quantitative information and your estimate of symbols performance will help us to make better maps'. With that kind of introduction subjects are not only likely to see their own performance in a different context but are also more likely to come forward with informal suggestions which may be of crucial value, more so than they would after a 'test' of their 'reaction'.

In this case there are even further ambiguities. The instructions go on to say 'Simply express as accurately as you can what the *values of the circle* are in comparison to the *standard circle* given' (ibid., p. 67). The term 'value' is not explained and could refer to area, diameter or perhaps some vague notion of size. The point is that subjects are free to employ a number of different strategies. The only one which is deliberately excluded in the instructions is the estimation of radius and the subsequent multiplication by pi to derive area. This is presumably excluded by the instruction, 'Do not complicate your judgment by applying geometric theorems'. Certainly I would find the above operation far less complicated than trying to estimate the 'values of the circles' out of thin air under 'test' conditions. None the less subjects still have two obvious strategies available to them — an estimate of 'value' based on diameter or an estimate based on a vague notion of size. There may well be others — estimating the length of the circumference or counting squares by imposing an imaginary square grid. Since none of these are excluded it is impossible simply on the basis of the resulting estimates to decide which strategy has been used. Whichever strategy is used, it cannot simply be a matter of 'perception' in a biological sense but must be partly dependent on the repertoire of strategies available to subjects and their estimates as to which is likely to yield the best results.

Researchers have assumed the task to be perceptual rather than cognitive and in doing so consistently underestimate the variety of possible options which may be open to map readers. Even though the visual skills of most will be poorly developed there is no doubt that intense training and dedication can result in extraordinary abilities to estimate size and scale by eye. The drawing by Volterra (Figure 34) is an impressive example of how the Renaissance artists learned to

Figure 34: Drawing by Daniele de Volterra (1599 - 1666)

Source: The Trustees of the British Museum.

make very competent judgements of scale with the aid only of what current researchers regard as a rather crude instrument — the human eye — but which Volterra and his contemporaries regarded as their most acute form of intelligence which could be improved throughout a lifetime of practice. There is a world of difference between this drawing of a foot and a circle on a map, but they are linked by the process used in their execution and understanding.

Given the 'vision' of current researchers, the achievement of the artist is simply impossible. The humbleness of the task of map reading should not blind us to the flexibility and power of the instrument used. Nevertheless the problems of using circles on maps are not practically resolvable by ten years of dedicated apprenticeship to a Renaissance master! One obvious solution is not to use circles at all; but against this is the considerable practical advantage they have over other graphic forms on maps (Meihoefer, 1969). It is simpler to transpose data into circles than into other statistical mapping techniques, it takes less time to draw circles than other symbols, and finally circles are more efficient users of map space. These factors have combined to make them attractive to map makers despite their disadvantages to the user. Thus the human and graphic resolution of the problem is determined by economic consideration. The solution to the problem, as it turns out, is remarkably simple (Meihoefer, 1973). By presenting map readers with a scale set of circles identical with those used on the map, errors dropped to zero! We can see why this is so when we consider the task. Users are not being asked to make an estimation of a change in value (whatever that may be); they are now required to match one circle with another, so that vague estimation is replaced by precise matching. It is doubtful that these two situations are even comparable as they involve very different kinds of tasks and hence require very different kinds of skill.

The conclusion we are drawn to, yet again, is that a more sensitive understanding of the user's requirements for the task can lead to effectiveness. Perhaps the result could have been obtained more speedily and efficiently if researchers had begun with a close and detailed observation of the task rather than the 'testing' of subjects. In case it may seem that these are the same thing, I would hasten to distinguish between what we might characterise as an ethnography of communciation as opposed to a laboratory investigation of communication. It is significant that the latter is far more popular than the former, among researchers, partly because of the misguided view that it is more scientific; it is certainly likely to lead to work which is more publishable.

As with professional communicators, the primary career commitment among researchers is to peer group standards with the eventual user taking second place. This has to be seen not as an aspect of the logic of scientific research but as the product of the institutional environment in which the research is conducted. The consequence in this case was that a successive series of quantitative studies which failed to pay careful attention to the task were responsible for alternately misleading and overcomplicating the enquiry. The eventual solution was a qualitative change in the task itself.

A curious feature of much of this and similar research in graphic communication is the simple framework which is used to describe results. Typically data is divided into correct and incorrect reponses. On occasion the magnitude of error is recorded but there the analysis stops. No attempt is made to determine whether all errors are due to the same reasons or whether they represent a range of qualitatively different responses. Any notion of the audience which might involve a complex, cognitively-based system cannot be entertained because the form in which the data is collected fails to capture differences which may be due to such a system.

In order to aid future research in this area we need a new approach which acknowledges at the outset the possibility that there may well be more than one way to approach any particular graphic task. One should not even assume at the outset that the task is understood or that the only use to which the material may be put is the one specified by the researcher. Research should begin with an open-ended investigation, the purpose of which is to generate alternative uses and styles of usage of the graphic material. Care should always be taken to draw on the knowledge of at least three distinct groups; the experienced graphic practitioner, the experienced user and the user with no experience. The emphasis throughout should be on asking for advice and help, not testing reactions. Sensitivity and imagination are far more useful at this stage than rigour and precision; many problems and insights will present themselves and there are occasions when the logic of the task, as revealed through this kind of study, points to solutions without the need to go any further.

One can never lose sight of the fact that considerable time and money can be spent on research which may not in the end yield a definite solution. As I have repeatedly indicated, the extent of control that an instructional designer has over the learner via the instructional material is due to co-operation and expectations of the learner, not to any intrinsic quality of the material. It may well be that a preliminary investigation of this kind will reveal no clear solution and one may have to admit that no control is possible. Only when this preliminary phase is exhausted and some possible solutions look likely is it then worth investigating a small sample of the potential users. Once again the emphasis should be on qualitative rather than quantitative research. At all times the users should be acquainted with the nature of the enquiry and be encouraged to offer opinions and advice; particular attention should be paid to the normal expectations of the learner and the way in which the graphic material is contextualised by the supporting material, the course or the environment in which the material is used. An army recruit in a training camp is in a very different environment to the housewife in her own kitchen or the claimant in a social security office. Learning can and does take place in all of these locations, but it is doubtful whether it is motivated in the same way, or guided by the same expectations and assumed consequences. More importantly, it is doubtful whether it draws on the same set of skills and knowlege. Only as a final resort, and only when quantitative comparisons will determine a particular choice, is it worth proceeding with rigorous investigations under controlled conditions. The outcome, however far down this road one travels, should be a greater understanding of the learner's problems, not a paper for publication, and the emphasis should be on local needs, not universal generalisations. For this to occur requires not any new and elaborate methodology but an institutional framework that will endorse and reinforce this kind of activity, one which will inhibit the rush to the laboratory. Such a framework will be amongst the considerations in the final chapter.

Diagrams and Thinking

I have constantly sought to elaborate the way in which vision is inseparable from intellectual activity. The emphasis so far has been on the student as the user of material produced by others; we have not considered the intellectual value to the learner of engaging in the process of producing material. Any system of communication is also a system for extending reflection. Visual thinking — the manipulation of our visible world to generate meaning — is both a hidden internal process and something which can be extended into material form; in other words, it can take place on paper or in model-building as an extension of internal thinking activity. Visual communication is the public manifestation of private reflection.

The advantages of external cognition are amply and spectacularly demonstrated by the history of science. The examples of Descartes, Kekulé and Watson and Crick have already been mentioned but the catalogue of achievements which depended intimately on the use of externalised visual thinking is extraordinarily large. When one begins to examine the history of science and ideas with the intention of seeking out those individuals who used visual thinking as an important part of their work, not only are the examples numerous but they shed an entirely new light on the progress of scientific thought. Sadly the literary emphasis in our culture has obscured this history and there are few documented accounts of the intimate link between the availability or invention of graphic devices and the development of scientific thinking. An exception to this is the study by Ann Harleman Stewart of graphic representation of models in linguistic theory which shows the relation between the introduction and development of graphic models and the progress of linguistic theory. She concludes:

> It is clear that as long as graphic representation furnishes linguistic science with models, as long as it influences the development of linguistic theory, the solution to the problems of model-building lies in more model-building. (Stewart, 1976)

If this conclusion is generally true of all scientific theories that use graphic techniques as part of theory construction, where do we find the emphasis for this in our education system? In what way do we encourage the young undergraduate to develop the intellectual habit of model-building (using that term in its broadest sense to cover both conceptual and two-or three-dimensional models)? It is a standard part of all science training to arm students with certain techniques of scientific discovery — the experimental method with all its attendant paraphernalia of equipment and statistical methods — but theory construction, which must be one of the most powerful tools of discovery, is left as a vague *ad hoc* area at the mercy of capricious commodities like creativity or genius. While not wishing to diminish the importance of excellence in human thought, theory construction does not occur intuitively. Indeed Stewart shows systematically, that theoretical advances owe much to the range of models available to the enquirer and the sophistication with which they are applied. What matters initially is whether a particular process of model construction is regarded as legitimate. If the process of model-making were — like the scientific method — a regular part of the teaching of scientists this would legitimate its use and provide scientists with a wider range of heuristic devices. Nothing illustrates this more clearly than the discovery in 1953 of the structure of DNA by Watson and Crick. The information on which they based their model was well known to the scientific community, but model-building, as Watson recounts in *The Double Helix*, was generally considered a rather unimportant activity. This gives us some insight into the attitude prevalent within our culture towards vision as an intellectual process in science. It was somehow not quite respectable to play with models. It was known that DNA was in some way involved in the duplication of genetic material in cell growth and in the transmission of genetic information from one cell to another. The chemical composition of DNA was also known, and it was possible to calculate the angles at which the various atoms were likely to join each other. It was not known, however, that the three-dimensional form of DNA was actually the basis for its capacity to reproduce itself accurately, until Watson and Crick, despite prevailing attitudes, constructed a model according to the known data. What was not apparent from the chemical and mathematical inform-ation was readily apparent once the model had been constructed, namely, that the mechanism of genetic tranmission is effected by a double helix (spiral), one side of which passes information to the other. Model-building is now quite respectable among biochemists, and the range of model-building techniques has greatly advanced since Watson and Crick painstakingly soldered short pieces of metal one to another; but the more general lesson remains to be learnt: it is still the case that the training of scientists does not include a visual education which would greatly enhance the range of conceptual tools available to them. The importance of the discovery of DNA structure in this context is that it resulted from the transformation of the invisible into the visible by the use of a visual metaphor.

In another branch of science, physics, we can seen how a theory using diagrams is preferred over mathematical forms. In 1948 Richard Feynman and Julian Schwinger independently developed a quantum theory of electrons and photons. However in contrast to Schwinger's conventional mathematical account, Feynman expressed the complicated mathematical expressions in the form of diagrams which contain visually the same information as the original mathe-matics. It was this way of presenting his results that led to the rapid acceptance of Feynman's theory and to further important advances.

Figure 35 represents visually the complex mathematical expression of the scattering of two electrons by the exchange of photons. The electrons are represented by the solid lines and the photons by the wiggly lines (Storer and Cahill, 1978).

Figure 35: Feynman's Diagram

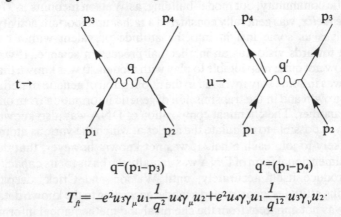

$$q = (p_1 - p_3) \qquad\qquad q' = (p_1 - p_4)$$

$$T_{fi} = -e^2 u_3 \gamma_\mu u_1 \frac{1}{q^2} u_4 \gamma_\mu u_2 + e^2 u_4 \gamma_\nu u_1 \frac{1}{q^{12}} u_3 \gamma_\nu u_2.$$

Charles Sanders Peirce, the American logician and father of American semiotics, devoted the later part of his life to the development of a system of diagrammatic thinking to fundamental logic. It is significant that a man who devoted much of his life trying to understand our systems of communication saw his work with diagrams as potentially the most useful of his many achievements in furthering human understanding. It is only recently that Peirce's scattered thoughts on this subject have been organised systematically after eighty years of neglect (Roberts, 1973) and we have yet to see the application of these ideas to contemporary thought.

All of these uses of diagrams in abstract thinking and theory construction are isolated incidents, happy consequences of serendipity. They do not flow from a systematic knowledge of the power of diagrams. Some aspects of diagrams are part of mathematical reasoning (Euclidian geometry must be the best example), but there is no comparison between the universal and coherent acknowledgement of the value of mathematics in the process of understanding and the fragmented and haphazard use of diagrams. We have neither a history nor a theory of diagrams. The elements of such a discipline are in the making. Stewart's work, already mentioned, is a useful model which may well serve in the investigation of the history of diagrams in other disciplines, and there are some useful insights in two recent papers (Garland, 1979; Macdonald-Ross, 1979). What is necessary is a formal analysis of diagrams, a psychological account of their use, an historical study of their development and a review of their current status in our culture. This last is extremely important when it comes to introducing them in education. I have found that students vary in their approach to diagrams. Humanities students unacquainted with diagrams can become very uneasy when diagrammatic explanations are offered instead of verbal explanations. This may be due in part to simple unfamiliarity but it may also be due to a basic antipathy to something which looks scientific or more profoundly to an inability to make the cognitive transformation from diagram to object. There is also the more general problem, which we observed in relation to drawings, of the diagram traditionally having an unequivocal place in the text. It is not usual for a controversy to be rehearsed diagrammatically. More often than not any debate or argument is carried on in verbal form, with diagrams summarising or confirming the conclusion. Once again we are led back to the central role of existing expectations and how it is necessary to change those expectations in order to make full use of diagrams.

An enthralling aspect of the expectations of diagrams in the history of ideas, which has perhaps been forgotten or which sits uneasily on the fringes of contemporary intellectual life, is to be found in the art of mnemonics. Frances A. Yates has brought to light an intellectual tradition dating from ancient Greece, which remained one of the major scholarly skills up to about 300 years ago when it declined concurrently with the rise of science (Yates, 1978). Mnemonics, the art of memory, is not a feature of contemporary life with our libraries and data banks and the information explosion, but in prior ages when orators and lawyers had to memorise speeches, statutes and legal precedents without immediate recourse to texts, the art of memory flourished. The principle, the discovery of which is attributed to the Greek poet Simonides, is remarkably simple. We have a natural ability to remember places and buildings and we recall a great deal of specific detail. It is possible, mentally as it were, to go for a walk round such a location. The art of memory consists essentially of placing the things we wish to remember in specific 'locations' along the route. In order to retrieve them all one has to do is return to that 'place' and find them there. It may sound absurdly simple but it does work; practice and many centuries of accumulated strategies resulted in a powerful intellectual process which was an essential ingredient of scholarship.

It was realised within this long history that the building or location did not have to be real. The essence of the skill was initially to memorise a structure which could serve as a suitable framework for memorising facts. That structure could be an imaginary building, model or diagram. At their most sophisticated, the mnemonicists realised that the framework should in some manner reflect the structure of the knowledge they wished it to contain. In this way the diagram or imaginary building took on a metaphysical significance, becoming eventually a formal metaphor for the structure of all things, and providing a link between mnemonics and philosophy, particularly with the hermetic philosophies associated with mysticism. There is of course a long association between diagrams and various occult and mystical systems of thought, many of which were connected with the memorising of secret or special knowledge.

Thus there is a long history of using diagrams for some of the most profound and obscure of human purposes. A recent work, though in many ways detached from its antecedents, picks up these ancient themes of the nature of man and existence and explores them through diagrams (Albarn and Smith, 1977). It has all the grandeur, breadth of vision and impenetrable obscurity of the cabala but it contains the germ of a very important idea which is the central point of this section:

> The diagram is evidence of an idea being structured — it is not *the idea* but a model of it, intended to clarify characteristics of features of that idea. It is a form of communication which increases the pace of development, or allows an idea to function and develop for the thinker while offering the possibility of transfer of an idea or triggering of notions: finally through appropriate structuring, it may generate different notions and states of mind in the viewer. (ibid., p. 7)

The intellectual potential of diagrams still lies before us largely unexplained in any systematic fashion, its history uncharted, its formal basis yet to be mapped out and most significantly its educational potential untapped.

In Chapter 6 (p. 106) I introduced Duchastel's three roles of instructional illustration. The final role Duchastel calls 'retentional' and describes thus:

> Illustrations in this role are presumed to act somewhat as do section headings, that is to say, they form a conceptual plan of the

subject matter for the learner, although an iconic plan rather than a verbal one. It is through this plan that memory is facilitated. During later recall, the student can initially retrieve from memory the iconic representations of the topics which were presented in the text, and through these he or she gains immediate access to their verbal representation.

He also says: 'This role is derived from theory and remains to be supported by instructional research' (Duchastel, 1978, p. 38).

It is a sad reflection on the narrowness of much of the current writing in educational technology that an entire tradition is simply ignored because it does not feature in the educational research literature. There is a grave danger of reinventing the wheel. The point is, however, simple enough. For centuries people have made and used visual communication. Even though our technology is new, our symbolic systems have been a long time in the making. Before we rush to the laboratory we should extend to our 'primitive' forebears the courtesy of asking them what they discovered through practice that may be of use to us now.

9 TYPOGRAPHY — THE HIDDEN ORDER

Introduction

Typography is the art of designing or choosing typefaces and organising their position on the page. It is at the heart of the most common form of visual communication — the printed word. Typography as a distinct profession emerged with the changes in printing technology that began in the nineteenth century. The introduction of photography and mechanical punch-cutting of letter forms meant an enormously increased range of choices, and at the same time printing processes became more complex and varied, so that printers, who traditionally made typographic decisions, became more specialised. This left a gap. The production process was capable of great diversity and there was a need to consider as a separate problem the rational basis of decision-making when choosing the best design for any particular purposes. The first typographers were also master printers, but as we observed in relation to engineering drawing, complexity and sophistication in the production process separated out the various roles so that eventually there emerged a distinct planning role which could take an overview of the process. In the printing industry this meant that the decisions relating to a particular printing job were made with a perspective involving many other jobs, possibly encompassing the entire output of a printing works or publishing house. It was out of this planning function that typographic design evolved.

There can hardly be an establishment of tertiary education which does not have some printing facility at its disposal. There are, however, many that do not recognise the need for special advice on typographic decisions, which is unfortunate, because as I hope this chapter will make clear, typographic design is an important aspect of visual communication. Its consequences for education are both economic and pedagogic. Sound practice in typographic design can result in significant economies, though pedagogic gains in typography as in other aspects of communication remain more elusive and difficult. A recent contribution to the literature (Hartley, 1978) offers sound guidance on economic matters but as a recent review argues (Kinross, 1979), it consistently flounders when trying to offer educational advice. Most of the attempts to understand typography and its relation to the reader, using rigorous experimental methods, have been superfluous. The most important problems in understanding this relationship are conceptual. Accordingly,and consistently with earlier chapters, I shall devote most of my observations to how we think about typography in relation to learning.

Typography as Stimulus

The main thrust of my criticism of the research methods used in the investigation of communication in education will by now be familiar to the reader, but at the risk of being tiresome I will repeat the main points because they are particularly pertinent to typography which has held a special allure for experimental psychologists.

First, the research assumes that the message can be treated as a separate unit of analysis independent of the author or the audience, whereas I have suggested that the basic units should be the author/ message relation and the audience/message relation. Secondly, and often despite theoretical pretensions to the contrary, experimental methods are devised that implicitly treat the audience as passive organisms rather than as active social beings. Thirdly, the role of schemata and the variety and complexity of transformations that the learner can use are neglected often in favour of very crude categoris- ation and measurement of responses, which leaves out considerations of meaning and inferred authorship and audiences. Finally, the process of objectification, both as a source of error and as a powerful force in preserving meanings, is ignored.

All of these faults can be readily seen in typographic research. Of all the areas of investigation in this text, typography has suffered most from a relentless and often mindless investigation of the relation between typographic variables and human performance. The reasons why typography has been singled out by researchers are doubtless due to the fact that typographic variables (such as point size, spacing, line width and margin) are themselves easily measurable and therefore seem to lend themselves peculiarly well to the setting up of controlled experiments in which typographic variables are studied individually in relation to human performance. The most outstanding contributor to this kind of research has been Miles A. Tinker (Tinker, 1965). His work consistently reflects a choice of inappropriate units of analysis. Treating the material qualities of the message as separate both from the typographer as author and from the reader as audience, effectively neutralises any value this type of research might have. As Hartley, in his recent book, reluctantly has to admit:

> Unfortunately, however, the research in these areas is not very helpful to designers of instructional materials, principally because such variables as typesize, line-length and interline space have been studied independently of the typographic design of highly structured information. (Hartley, 1978, p. 20)

Although Hartley clearly recognises the perils of separating out the message in this way, he continues to do so and his recommendations for the evaluation of educational material are consistent with this separation. Even when these inappropriate research techniques do yield usable generalisations, mainly about legibility and reading efficiency as summarised by Spencer (Spencer, 1969), Hartley is forced to admit that: 'The research literature does offer some generalisations but such advice to printers hardly seems world-shattering' (ibid., p. 109).

A closer scrutiny of the actual studies on which these generalisations are based reveals, first, that many of them are negative in the sense that they have discovered *no* difference in legibility attributable to specific typographic variables; and secondly, that where differences have been discovered the picture is far from clear-cut because there is always some overlap in the performance of individual subjects tested under the different conditions. It is vital to distinguish between an *important* difference and the often used technical statistical notion of 'significant difference'. The latter term merely indicates that the difference between two groups of results is unlikely to be due to chance factors; it does not say whether that difference is small or large. Most results in typographical research show small differences with considerable overlap between groups subjected to different conditions.

It is not surprising therefore that many professional typographers are sceptical, even contemptuous, of the psychological research in their field. The treatment of typography as stimulus in laboratory investigations has not been very productive and its advocates have failed to demonstrate its usefulness to typographic practice.

It nevertheless remains the case that typographers are genuinely interested in the needs of readers whether those readers are the general public or more specialised groups such as students; there is a long and admirable tradition in typography of unobtrusive dedication to the needs of the reader. As a leading typographer of this century put it:

Typography may be defined as the art of rightly disposing printing material in accordance with specific purpose; of so arranging the letters, distributing the space and controlling the type as to aid to the maximum the reader's comprehension of the text . . . any disposition of printing material which, whatever the intention, has the effect of coming between author and reader is wrong. (Morison, 1967, p. 5)

Typographers are in a very real sense artists of a hidden order. Typography is deeply embedded within the fabric of our culture and it is from that perspective that we can begin to gain some insight into how, without recourse to experimental methods, the typographer can put into practice his commitment to the audience/message relation.

Typography as Social Practice

Typography is an extension of language and, as I have said before, language is the most homogeneous and standardised system of communication in any culture. The rules of usage related to any particular language are public in the widest sense. It is the sharing of those rules that gives the typographer a unique rapport with the audience; no other communications practitioner in a mass medium can claim such certainty of knowledge of the audience. This is mainly due to the singular position language enjoys, but it must also be due in part to the fact that printing is the oldest mass medium and centuries of trial and error have gone into the typographical conventions of our time. We should never forget that the reader is a highly trained user of printed matter whose training is conducted through social institutions. It is therefore surprising that psychologists should be considered as the most appropriate students of typography. Cultural practices are usually studied by anthropologists, or perhaps cultural analysts. It is clear that recently productive research in typographic audience/ message relations is of this kind, though this is not explicitly acknowledged by those who are engaged in it (Wright, 1979); but it is the case that the techniques which are being used, such as critical appraisal, field studies and interviews are more usually associated with anthropology and cultural studies than they are with experimental psychology. It is also interesting to note where some of the later research is being focused — in precisely those areas where new social practices have resulted in the need for new typographical conventions for which there is no specific precedent for either the typographer or the reader. Bureaucratic and technical institutions are relative newcomers but they have made extensive demands on typographers to design forms, technical publications and ways of simplifying or systematising complex procedures and statements. We are witnessing the development of a new social practice though one which is peculiarly aggravated by the inevitable gap between author and audience which is the distinguishing feature of large bureaucratic organisations. The printed word is very often the interface between organisations and the public. The typographer who designs this material is under great pressure to make things work in an area of uncertain conventions for people with widely different expectations and abilities. The problems and solutions are social.

Earlier in this century the problem was first translated into a social role by the German philosopher and sociologist Otto Neurath. Within the general framework of liberal democratic ideals Neurath believed that to be able to participate fully in the democratic process, the citizen needed to be adequately informed about economic and demographic facts. Unfortunately the normal way of presenting this information in the form of tables, graphs and written reports makes the information indigestible or simply inaccessible to the majority. The problem is similar to the one which afflicts government departments that wish to inform citizens of their rights in relation to claims and benefits, or to the problems of the educator in conveying complex and new information to the student. All have in common the need to transform information and to do so in a context where there is no explicit set of conventions to guide either the author or the reader. Neurath was commissioned in 1924 to design the displays of an exhibition which would inform citizens of Vienna of the economic and demographic facts shaping their lives. This led to the creation of a new role, the transformer — someone who mediates between specialist and the public. Neurath's work led to the foundation of the ISOTYPE movement which pioneered the graphic communication of economic, demographic, social and scientific information in a didactic context. This work represents one of the most significant contributions to visual communication in the twentieth century and should be studied by all practitioners in the field.

For a typographer to become a transformer requires a change in both the traditional philosophy of the unobtrusiveness of the typographer and in the range of responsibilities which the job entails. The typographer must either directly or with the aid of specialist researchers reach out to the audience to discover its needs, expectations and abilities; he must reach back to the author and if need be change, delete, add or restructure information; he must, if necessary, become visible to the audience.

All of these role changes require changes in the roles of those other people who work alongside the typographer or who use his product; this is why typography is best seen as a social practice. What has been said here about typographers is applicable in a more general sense to all professional communicators but as elsewhere the limiting factors in any communication process is ultimately the audience and we need to consider in more detail the audience/message relation in typography.

Reading as Social Practice

It is typical of most experimental studies of typography that variability in reading activity is either ignored or eliminated by statistical averaging procedures. Most studies do not investigate in any detail the strategies of reading and comprehension used by individual subjects. By contrast it is typical of experimental studies of reading that typographic variables are ignored. This means that there are two quite distinct traditions of audience/message research in relation to print, one focusing on typography and the other on the reading task. What to the reader is a composite task, to researchers is, oddly, divided. This unreal division also masks some very serious problems which lie in the way of progress in our understanding of the audience/message relation.

Reading research in its applied form can boast one of the most spectacular gains in efficiency in visual communication practice:

... when tested on short passages, [most people] can increase their reading speed by about 50 per cent, usually with better comprehension. But in real situations the tasks of reading, taken as a whole, are complex: the reader has to plan and organise, to select the best method for particular purposes — in short, to use a strategy of reading. (De Leeuw and De Leeuw, 1965, p. 10)

A difference of 50 per cent is enough to swamp any typographic variable; but more importantly reading is here regarded not as a simple response but as a complex learnt acitivity; in other words it is a social practice. We learn to read according to social assumptions about that task, and one of the assumptions that we have inherited as a consequence of centuries of typographic and reading practice is that typography is unobtrusive. When reading we attend to the words and apart from such cues as punctuation, paragraphing, chapters and possibly contents and index, the rest can be ignored. It is therefore hardly surprising that experiments conducted to measure differences in typographic variables as they relate to reading should be so disappointing. The subjects are at best operating at the fringes of their normal awareness of the reading task as it is *socially* defined. Put another way, the reading schema is one which ignores typography. From the point of view of a typographer faced with a wealth of choices it may seem that any particular choice *must* make a difference to the reader. But many of the more recent choices available to typographers are not due to centuries of trial and error: the superfluity of choices in typeface, typesize, spacing and layout are the by-products of the extremely flexible new technical process of photosetting. The fact that a choice may be available does not in any way make that choice desirable, let alone noticeable or usable by a reader with no awareness of the variations or their possible significance. At a certain level typographic choices are like the choices of Buridan's ass: faced with two equally attractive haystacks the ass was unable to decide between them and starved. There may well be typographic choices which seem extremely difficult and perplexing precisely because there are no behavioural criteria on which to base the choice between them.

There is also the possibility that, like a good piece of music, a well-designed piece of typography will reveal different facets of its composition on successive re-readings so that the reader's appreciation of the content and its form is constantly renewed and enhanced. But there is one prerequisite which is as important to music as to typography. The reader (or listener) must be aware that such complexity and intricacy is possible. In most contexts of reading the typographer is in no position to alter the relation between text and reader because that is a social practice outside his control in which he is embedded along with the reader.

Education, however, is different to the extent that learning is itself a process of change; the reader who expects to learn may be more receptive to advice about strategies for reading. If a text has been designed to reflect the structure of a complex argument or body of knowledge, the learner is more likely to comprehend the material if he or she is also aware of the typographical structure which has been used.

Rethinking the typographer's role in this way is an important departure from tradition. It needs to be matched by subtle changes in the institutional structures in which typographers work and it is towards this overall role of visual communication within institutions of learning that we turn in the final chapter.

10 THE FUTURE OF VISUAL EDUCATION

Introduction

In this, the final chapter, I want to bring together the various strands of argument that have been developed throughout this book. My main purpose, at this stage, is to translate those arguments into concrete policy proposals and suggest ways in which some of the deficiencies in current practice might be remedied and how it might be possible to plan for a better future.

Many educationalists may be concerned that certain omissions from the usual range of topics in this area are apparent in this text. Television and film, for example, have so far only been mentioned in passing; and there is no detailed discussion of objectives and evaluation. I shall begin with an explanation of these omissions. The key to any change in the way we think about visual communication lies in the restructuring of the institutional roles of those involved. I will suggest that some of the main problems in present practice are a consequence of outmoded institutional structures and certain mis-guided emphases in skills and career commitments in educational technology. This will lead to a consideration of the future training of those who will be most intimately involved in the development of visual communication in learning. The backbone of training and continued excellence must be an active and healthy research com-munity. I will suggest some fresh directions that may be fruitful. Finally I will consider in more general terms the future of visual communication in education.

Luminous Sundials?

An examination of most courses in educational technology reveals a massive concentration on educational objectives and evaluation. In Chapter 5, I argued that this emphasis gives a false impression of the degree of control over learning. Because the evaluator cannot describe either the media of education or the relationship between those media and learning in anything but the crudest terms, the important central link in the chain of events from objectives to

172

evaluation is simply not there. No refinement in taxonomies of objectives or statistical testing procedure will alter that. But the criticism goes much deeper. The purpose of educational objectives and evaluation here is to *predict* the consequences of visual communication. Unless we accept as evidence of success in this area the rather simplistic prediction that students can learn from the media, it still remains to be demonstrated that the attempt is worthwhile; I think it unlikely that we will ever see that demonstration. It is not that I regard those involved as lacking in skills or sophistication. If that was all that stood in the way, we should, after twenty years of considerable effort and expenditure, have seen some breakthroughs — but we have not. We have elaborate taxonomies and debates about taxonomies, we have no end of methodologies for testing student performance; but we still end up playing hunches and in the main following routine production techniques with no more predictive validity than we could have mustered twenty years ago. In short I am suggesting that the whole enterprise may well have been pointless.

But it is important to understand why, otherwise we are apt to repeat the mistakes for a further twenty years, getting better only at self-delusion. 'Scientific' procedures cannot work because the systems under investigation are governed by meanings and rules relating to meaning which cannot be reduced to cause and effect contingencies. The only way such a system can be controlled is by regulating the meanings in the system and the rules governing their usage. This is what we partially do with language and language learning, but as is clear from most of the areas we have examined in this book, control of meanings is diffused within the culture, refracted by personal experience and focused differently within different contexts, all of which are only marginally controlled by the education process. If meanings are not shared they are liable to be unpredictable, and if they are shared prediction is unnecessary. The attempt at the scientific design of instructional systems may well be like an attempt to design a luminous sundial. It is for those reasons that I have little to say about objectives and evaluation.

It is none the less important to seek ways to *understand* the relation between media and learning. I am here deliberately drawing a distinction between prediction and understanding. We are dealing with the symbolic world of consciousness where empathy, shared experience and common meanings — in short, understanding — are essential tools of analysis, and I am contrasting this with the world of inexorable physical processes where precision and control are the necessary tools for analysis and prediction. We have no formal methodology in education for such a 'soft' activity as understanding, but what I am suggesting is not in any way revolutionary. It is almost platitudinous to say that in order to teach well we need to understand our students. How could it be otherwise? There is an unbridgeable gulf between understanding students and predicting responses, and there is no methodology for human sensitivity and understanding. It is possible, though, with judicious planning to create an environment in which it might flourish, to which I will turn later in this chapter.

Missing Media

It would be impossible in a book of this kind to be comprehensive but some may disagree with my choices and wonder why I have not emphasised film and television which may be said to be significant media of visual communication. If one were to judge in economic terms, film and particularly television have taken a very large slice of the educational media cake. There is no shortage of advocates for televison and during the boom years of the sixties there was certainly no shortage of salesmen ready to install a full studio and OB unit at the drop of a requisition. Much of that equipment sits today in cupboards collecting dust. Some of it has found a place on the fringes, particularly in areas where remote, delayed or feedback learning are of value. For example, some experiments or clinical procedures which may be inaccessible or difficult for a whole class to observe can be observed remotely on television. Feedback on performance in sport, group dynamics and classroom practice are also useful areas. Here the medium is performing a task that clearly was not even conceivable before television. But in the wider areas of education it would be difficult to suggest that television or any of the other high technology media have swept aside the more traditional tools of the trade. A reasonable way to check the balance of media usage in education is to look at the study timetable of students (both formal and informal) to find out how much of the time is spent in various communication activities. Apart from interpersonal communication, the most time will be spent with books; television or film will in most courses account for very little time. It is partly for that reason that I have chosen the emphasis in this book.

There are other more subtle reasons why these media receive no detailed attention here. Most of the history of film and television is a history of popular entertainment. Most of the conventions developed by film-makers are narrative conventions; that is they have been worked out for purposes of dramatic and evocative story-telling. Even when they turn to non-narrative subjects as in current affairs, documentaries and science, the tendency to use narrative devices still predominates (Jones *et al.*, 1978). This means that subjects which may not necessarily warrant a narrative treatment are pressed into a narrative mould.

Because of the relatively brief history of these forms, and their predominant use, there is as yet no developed tradition of analytic discourse of a purely filmic or televisual kind. There is no reason in principle why such discourses should not be developed. As media for logical or empirical analysis, they may have extraordinary untapped potential, but this needs to be developed out of the existing narrative conventions by a kind of research yet to be undertaken which I shall turn to when dealing with research priorities.

At present these conventions place a limit on the usefulness of these media in education, a limit reinforced by the kinds of expectations most of us have of these forms as entertainment. Thus it is not sufficient only to make serious programmes; one must provide an audience with the necessary skills critically to evaluate the material. There have been some notable attempts at developing a critical vocabulary of film and television, particularly in the pages of *Screen* and *Screen Education*. This attempt has unfortunately suffered from a narrowness of purpose and a specialism of terminology which has made it inaccessible to anyone not familiar with contemporary Marxist theoretical debates, and of little appeal to anyone with broader interests than those revolving round ideology, its control and subversion. Nevertheless it marks an important beginning in the intellectualisation of film and television and the development of a serious critical language for the audience. To do full justice to this development would require far more space than is available here and would only be warranted if it were more widely used; for that to happen, it would require a basic shift in attitude towards these media and a substantial change in the economics of production (Schramm, 1977).

Unfortunately educationalists have been seduced by the popular prestige of these media into spending vast amounts on hardware. As Schramm puts it:

A visitor from another small planet unfamiliar with the atmosphere

which educational development takes place here, might be
[as]tonished to see how much of the effort and resources of a typical
project go into procuring and operating expensive hardware rather
than into producing more effective software (preferably for less-
expensive hardware). (ibid., p. 278)

I have no intention of bolstering this process further.

The Work of Visual Communication

The key to any change in the way we think about visual communication
does not lie in further research or rhetoric but in the way the
institutional structures legitimate the practice. I hope the arguments I
have offered show that there is a need to rethink the relation between
media and education. As I have emphasised repeatedly, visual
communication is a social practice; to alter it requires a change in the
supporting and sustaining social structure. In terms of educational
establishments this means some careful attention to job descriptions,
career prospects, professional bodies, departmental structures and
budgetary systems.

The best job description of the visual communication of the future
is contained in the notion of the Transformer, originally advanced by
Neurath, more recently articulated, with respect to textual material,
by Macdonald-Ross and Waller (1976). They offer this description:

He is the skilled professional communicator who mediates between
the expert and the reader. His job is to put the expert's message in a
form the reader can understand, and to look after the reader's
interest in general. (Macdonald-Ross and Waller, 1976, p. 142)

This is excellent as far as it goes, but it does not take account of the
way in which jobs are defined by institutions, not people, and usually
least of all by the person whose job it is. Thus when they exhort us to

break down the barriers in the interests of the reader. Take
responsibility for the success or failure of the communication. Do
not accept a label or a slot in a production line. Be a complete
human being with moral and intellectual integrity and thorough-
going technical competence. Be a transformer. (ibid., p. 152)

they do not seem to acknowledge that every 'production line' has a foreman and he, not as an individual but as a cog in the structure, defines the job. The consequence of bucking the system hardly needs spelling out.

Educational establishments are generally more flexible than factories but lone crusaders are not exactly welcome, particularly if their crusade involves changing the roles and responsibilities of others. A more satisfactory method of changing social roles is to change the structures in which they operate. In Chapter 3, I gave some account of the circumstances surrounding the work of professional communicators in the mass media. The dominant feature of their position is their almost total isolation from the audience. This is partly explicable in terms of the scale of the organisation but more particularly due to a separation of roles between production and audience research, a separation that goes back to the small-scale craft origins of all communication arts which only entailed skills of production as a definition of role. It is clear that this role needs to be changed so that both functions — production and audience research — can be integrated into the one individual, or at least into an enlarged view of the production process. It is also clear that traditional positivist research has not been very productive and that alternative styles of research more sympathetic to the meaningful nature of communication are necessary. The problem is not unique to communications but may be seen as a particular instance of organisational problem-solving and as such, Action Research may be a better framework. Much of my criticism of experimental procedures in visual communication is based on such a perspective (Susman and Evered, 1978).

To facilitate this change in direction requires a definite commitment to incorporating audience research as part of the production process. This means allocating time and funding, and specifying the specific stages within the production process when audience research should take place. The importance of these institutional allocations cannot be overemphasised. They, more than any fine sentiments, will change the way in which the process of communication is perceived by those engaged in it. The actual amount as a function of overall allocation in funding, should be somewhere between 10 and 20 per cent of production costs. These figures are based on informal estimates though there are some precedents (Lesser, 1974). Research should be programmed to the actual production sequences and should lead to the communicator having an awareness of the audience and the context in which the communication takes place, on the basis of some first-hand experience. The emphasis should be on informal first-hand encounters with the audience, *not* on structured experimental procedures. The latter should be used only as a last resort, if at all.

What has become apparent, from the areas of visual communication examined, is that the skilled practitioner is more likely to make sound judgements on the basis of years of experience than the positivist researcher on the basis of precise research. It is therefore imperative that the cumulative knowledge of practice be nurtured. Much weight is placed on publications when considering promotions or new appointments, which mitigates against the practitioner and in favour of the orthodox researcher. It also puts pressure on the practitioner to turn attention to this activity. If the quality of visual communication in education is to improve we must reinforce the development of practical skills over long periods of time.

Unfortunately, educational technology units, which are the ones most likely to contain the activities described in this book, are dominated by educational testing and hardware specialists, so the emphasis is on evaluation and hardware management. From all that I have said it should be apparent that this emphasis, while lending a quasi-respectability to a relatively new area, has not actually been very productive and it is now time to change direction and give emphasis to practitioners — the transformers of the future.

Research Priorities

My stress on practice should not be taken as a rejection of research in visual communication, only the rejection of a particular style of research. In order to develop and reinforce the strength of practical activity we need a sense of continuity with past efforts in visual communications. In other words we need an adequate history of the subject so that we can draw on the knowledge of the past. A recent and significant contribution in this area has been the work on the ISOTYPE movement at Reading University (Twyman, 1975). This kind of research needs to be encouraged, for as we have seen in relation to mnemonic aids, we are missing important ideas if we ignore the past.

We also need to sharpen our analytic tools. A great deal hinges on the way we describe the phenomenon of visual communication, and I have tried in the text to offer a critical contribution to our vocabulary in this area. Essentially we need to be able more fully to describe the audience/message relations of visual communication, which in part can be achieved by critical analysis of hypothetical audience/message relations as in content analysis. To understand how actual audiences relate to symbolic material ultimately requires empirical research but of a style quite different from present studies, one which can draw more on the semiotic quality of visual communication and less on its psychophysical qualities.

Our knowledge of visual communication practice is — like our knowledge of other design areas — lamentably inadequate. I have previously criticised the imbalance of research in this area (Sless, 1978) and have reported some research in this area that suggests that objectification may be a very powerful counterproductive force in effective communication (Sless, 1979), but this merely scratches the surface. I have drawn, in this text, on the sociology of mass communicators as an area of likely similarity to visual communications but we have no systematic knowledge of the working environment of the educational media producer. To be able to advise media producers on anything other than the technicalities of their activities requires some knowledge of the best kinds of institutional structures. In this chapter I have made a number of specific recommendations but at best they can only be regarded as a tentative move in the right direction.

We must never lose sight of the fact that visual communication is a constantly evolving practice. New technologies, new meanings and new areas of application are constantly emerging. There is a kind of research most frequently associated with art at the very frontiers of meaning that continually offers new ways of understanding. We should be ready to assist and encourage this most elusive area whenever we encounter it.

These areas of research are the essential intellectual base on which to build the superstructure of future visual communication practice. A sense of history, intellectual clarity, institutional role and new possibilities should be at the basis of practical training. Where it exists we must nurture it and where it is lacking we should make every effort to introduce it.

Visual Communication in General Education

It is fitting that this book should end with a plea on behalf of the audience — the student whom we all serve. Our educational culture has been dominated by the skills of literacy and numeracy. By contrast the overall culture in our societies is increasingly dominated by hybrid forms that use many visual forms of communication which our education system either ignores or simply takes for granted. The range of uses we can make of visual communication is always limited by the expectations of students. If our general education does not, in the formative years, develop and enlarge the expectations students have of visual material, we lose a potential method of understanding which higher education cannot fully take advantage of without engaging in remedial activity. Incorporating visual education into the general curriculum must be the long-term consequence of the realisation that vision is an intellectual process.

GLOSSARY

Audience/Message Relation, and Author/Message Relation. These are the two basic units in analysis of the communication process. It is argued in this text that the smallest indivisible unit of study in the communication process is either the audience/message relation or the author/message relation. It is impossible to reduce these relations to their component parts, investigate those parts as if they had a separate existence, and then reconstitute the components into the process of communication. These terms are used for the first time in this text, though many previous writers have made similar distinctions; Novitz for example greatly clarifies discussion about pictures by sharply distinguishing between pictures and pictorial representation (Novitz, 1977, pp. 5-10) which are roughly equivalent to author/message relations and audience/message relations respectively as used in this text. My formulation is to be preferred because it is more general and also because it is less open to ambiguous interpretation. Knowledge of the audience/message relation is very sparse. Most studies have been conducted in the behaviourist tradition, separating 'stimulus' and 'response', treating the relation simplistically as one of cause and effect. Much more is known about the author/message relation. The majority of critical writings in the arts have developed methods of scholarship in order to examine this relation. In literature studies, for example, there is no developed tradition of readership research; most discussion revolves around authorship and literary and cultural traditions, and their influence on writing. The term 'author' is used here in a general sense to describe any individual or group involved in making messages, and the term 'audience' in an equally general sense to describe all receivers of messages.

Code. A code is a systematic body of rules governing the generation of meaning. The most obvious example of this in everyday usage is the body of rules governing our language. Unfortunately many recent researchers have fallen into the trap of assuming that anything which can be described as meaningful must, like language, be governed by a commonly shared code. It remains an open empirical question as to how commonly shared any code may be. It is also logically possible for any message to be meaningful in terms

181

of a number of codes but there is no logical way of deciding independently of a particular audience/message or author/message relation what that code may be.

Communication. The term has been used so widely in recent years that it is no longer profitable to try to embrace all its senses. In this text communication is used in a restricted sense to cover all those situations in which meaning is generated with an explicit or implicit assumption of either an audience or an author. Communication is distinguished from information (see Chapter 2 for a full discussion).

Content Analysis. A formal methodology for analysing messages. It is useful to differentiate between two broad kinds of content analysis: quantitative and qualitative. The quantitative kind, applied most successfully to written text, provides a quantitative description of messages, usually by employing a set of categories into which different kinds of statements or parts of statements can be grouped, so that objectively comparable measurements between different messages can be made. Its roots are firmly within the positivist tradition of social science research. See Berelson for a classic text in this field (Berelson, 1952).

Qualitative content analysis has many roots in areas as diverse as art criticism, theology, linguistics and anthropology, all of which offer prescriptions for interpretation. Contemporary notions, generally grouped under such headings as structuralism or semiotics, seek to expose what they believe to be the underlying symbolic structure of any given message. Much of this work is difficult and frequently obscure. Its intellectual roots are in structural linguistics (de Saussure, 1974) and amongst the most influential thinkers on this style of analysis is a small group of French intellectuals of the post-war period (Sturrock, 1979). A typical example of the application of this general approach can be found in Fiske and Hartley (1978).

While these two forms of content analysis have different intellectual traditions there are a number of highly original and provocative hybrid studies that employ a mixture of both quantitative and qualitative methods. See for example Gerbner (1972).

All forms of content analysis are subject to a logical paradox because it is logically impossible to infer about audiences or authors from content analysis but equally it is impossible to engage in content analysis without making assumptions about authors or audience. No increase in sophistication of content analysis can remedy this basic flaw.

Description/Explanation. This contrasts two kinds of asssumptions which are made, both by authors and audiences, about the functions of messages. Descriptions are those messages which are assumed to contain material which is fundamentally intelligible to authors and audiences equally, so that the message is seen as a vehicle for transposing material from author to audience; thus a good description is one which tranposes material without loss of fidelity. By contrast an explanation is a message about which it is assumed by the author or the audience (or both) that the material contained is *not* equally intelligible to both parties and that the author is engaged in an act of transformation which makes that material intelligible to the audience. Thus a good explanation is one which transforms material from an unintelligible to an intelligible form. In actuality all messages involve transformation and therefore in a strictly technical sense description is a false notion. The fact that this false distinction exists is extremely important in the understanding of cultural processes.

Effectiveness. Most often used to describe a message which fulfils its purpose. It is a term which has strong positivist implications and tends to be associated with systems approaches where effectiveness is supposedly determined by measuring responses. It is also sometimes used as a synonym for 'powerful' — a message which is 'effective' may be a powerful or compelling message. In this text the usage is idiosyncratic and refers to those situations where an author from within the author/message relation is able to foresee and describe accurately the audience/message relation.

Gestalt. A German word meaning, roughly, form, structure, design, pattern, configuration or organised whole, where that whole is different from the mere sum of its parts. The Gestalt psychologists began in the second decade of this century to challenge the then atomist view of experience which considered experience to be composed of discrete units out of which complex wholes were made. The Gestalt psychologists argued on both empirical and philosophical grounds that experience could not be reduced to elements but must be regarded as a series of lawfully-structured patterns. Their ideas, particularly in perception, had an enormous influence on the theory behind contemporary art education, which has persisted in the training of graphic designers, although the theory has long been absorbed into the general history of psychology; its findings, though important, have not provided a lasting basis for understanding visual communication.

Inferred Audience. Every act of message construction by an author involves either an implicit or an explicit inference about an author. It is a feature of such inferences that the audience does not have to exist. It is only necessary that the author believes the audience to exist. Nor does the author have to be correct about an audience, only plausible, within the author/message relation. This concept grows out of many earlier ideas. It has some affinities with the term 'positioning' and 'appellation' as they have been applied in some forms of qualitative content analysis (Williamson, 1978), though the usage in this text is simpler and more precise as well as being less deterministic in its consequences.

Inferred Author. The parallel process to inferred audiences. Defining something within the audience/message relation as a message invokes the logical necessity of inferred authorship. Once again it is not necessary for the author actually to exist, it is only necessary for the audience to believe in the author's existence. This idea has its roots in many earlier notions and it can in principle assume many guises, from a specific individual to a notion of culture or society as author (Foucault, 1977).

Information. In order to make the term 'communication' usable by focusing its meaning into a specific area I have sought to make a distinction between information and communication. Anything of which we can become aware can be regarded as information. It is thus the term of greatest generality. By contrast communication is only that information to which we ascribe the property of being a message.

Meaning. This is an extremely difficult term with a long history of debate and philosophical analysis (Platts, 1979). It is a central term in the philosophy of language and deserves greater attention than can be given to it here. For the purposes of this text it is convenient to regard meaning as a complex term which covers many shades of its use. Meaning has mainly to do with the notion of 'standing for', not in a simple sense of 'one word, one object' but more in the sense of representing in the way than an ambassador can stand for his country's interests in another place and at times be there in his own right. Clearly this sense of representing is complex; I have deliberately chosen to use the analogy of an ambassador to give some sense of the complexity of the term. However, one feature of meaning should predominate for the purposes of this text and that is its relational quality. Meaning is *never* a property of objects but always a property of relationships. In taking this position we leave open the possibility which must always be considered in education that one person's meaning may be another person's misunderstanding; for there is nothing intrinsic to a message that absolutely determines its meaning.

Monosemic/Polysemic. These two terms represent a useful polarity between those situations where one particular meaning predominates (monosemic) and those situations where many meanings seem possible (polysemic). Typically one might contrast a workshop drawing with an abstract expressionist painting. However, in making these contrasts it is important to understand how much of these meanings are actually determined by the context of usage rather than the quality of the images. One must also beware of suggesting that even given a relatively controlled context the meaning is wholly monosemic. There is always a possibility of figurative overlay which is not controllable by proscription.

Objectification. This is a psychological process through which we externalise our own knowledge and expectations onto a message in such a way that we have the impression that the meaning is in the message rather than in the interaction between ourselves and the message. It is a process which helps to maintain, at an individual level, the stability of meaning. Its intellectual origins are in the psychological concept of projection and more recently in Gombrich's notion of 'the beholder's share' (Gombrich, 1960). I use the term 'objectification' in preference to these earlier terms in order to emphasise the peculiar but absolutely critical epistemological status given to the cognitive process. It should not be confused with the same term as applied in Marxist cultural theory where it has a slightly different meaning.

Optic Array. A term coined by the late J.J. Gibson, an eminent radical American psychologist, to describe the structure of ambient light in the environment. Most psychological theories of visual perception in this century have started from the assumption that light is a jumbled mass of energy from which the organism generates coherence. Gibson's radicalism in this respect was to invert the proposition and suggest that light itself is actually coherent — that is, as an organism moves through the environment the pattern of light from objects undergoes regular, systematic and predictable change, providing the organism with information which does not have to be interpreted and made coherent. Light already possesses coherence in the form of the optic array (Gibson, 1966).

Photographic Seeing. Because photographic picture-making is fundamentally non-selective — anything in front of the lens will be recorded on the film — photographers have had to develop the ability to see in a way which enables them to notice in the viewfinder certain features that would be ignored, or given different emphasis, in ordinary seeing.

Schema. This term has a long history but in its current use it owes much to the pioneer work of Bartlett (Bartlett, 1932) and more recently to Neisser (Neisser, 1976), who describes it thus:

> A schema is that portion of the entire perceptual cycle which is internal to the perceiver, modifiable by experience, and somehow specific to what is being perceived. (p. 54)

It should be noticed that a schema stands in a theoretical sense in opposition to the optic array; but it is only because both the optic array and schema come together that photographic seeing is possible. Schema enables us to deal with that aspect of perception which is determined by the structure of our retained past experience and present expectations. It is not a precise term but a very useful one.

Selective Attention. There is no doubt that attention is a most important aspect of education. Its importance as a basic aspect of how we perceive in general is also undeniable. Psychologists have searched for a mechanism that deals with selective attention — a sort of device that filters out unwanted information leaving us to attend to important stimuli. Neisser argues that such a mechanism does not exist (Neisser, 1976). His reasoning is elegantly simple: he argues that perception is an action, not an event; something we do, not something that happens to us.

> Attention is nothing but perception: we choose what we will see by anticipating the structural information it will provide. (p. 87)

Semiotics. Semiotics is the study of signs. Signs in this context mean anything which can be used to convey meaning, including such diverse cultural phenomena as language, pictures, fashion, architecture and ritual. At one time or another each of these (and many others) have been singled out as worthy objects of semiotic enquiry — the idea that these things are manifestations of a common human and cultural process is compellingly powerful, one which has gripped the imagination and interest of many thinkers and researchers of our time.

Not surprisingly, such an ambitious enterprise, which includes so much of the world within its scope, has not progressed without difficulty or controversy. The accumulation of fascinating ideas, which suggest the potential for many new insights and ways of understanding, also gives the misleading impression that semiotics is a well-established discipline with a body of theory, methods and findings. It would be more realistic to regard the extensive literature in the area as a debate about a possible subject. This is not readily apparent to newcomers, particularly if they begin with any of the basic or elementary texts on the subject.(See for example Barthes, 1967; Guiraud, 1975; Hawkes, 1977; Leach, 1976.) In these books, the style is assertive, overconfident: there is no debate about the ideas, only assertion, often with almost oracular overtones. It is necessary to go to more advanced texts before it becomes apparent that careful scholars are still sceptical about the fundamental issues of theory, methods and findings. (See particularly Sebeok 1976; Sturrock, 1979.) Some of the first premises of contemporary semiotics are open to criticism and doubt and accordingly many contemporary theorists are concerned with defining very basic notions.

Systems Approach. An extremely popular theoretical framework for examining complex phenomena. It tries to analyse the multiple interactions both on and within structures that display stability or continuity. The most powerful areas of application have been in the biological sciences and in computing. Its value in education has been largely to force educators to think systematically about what they do. It has not made education more controllable except in a limited technical and instrumental sense.

Visual Communication. Any form of communication that relies in part or whole on vision for its understanding.

Visual Literacy. This concept has arisen in many forms, not always under the same name. One aspect, which has its roots in Bauhaus teaching, is to be found in such works as Dondis's *A Primer in Visual Literacy* (Dondis, 1973). This view is essentially formal and consists of developing a greater sensitivity to the formal aspects of visual composition. A greater emphasis on practical communication skills is to be found in the ideas of Balchin and Coleman (Balchin and Coleman, 1965) where the rather inelegant term 'Graphicacy' is used. My own view is that visual literacy can include these approaches and others but basically it is a way of identifying any activity which is concerned with increasing the extent to which we regard all visual material and its uses as worthy of intelligent consideration.

ANNOTATED BIBLIOGRAPHY

Banham, Reyner. *Theory and Design in the First Machine Age* (The Architectural Press, London, 1960). A useful guide to some of the ideas which are at the foundation of contemporary philosophy of practice in design.

Barthes, Roland. 'Rhetorique de l'Image', *Communications*, vol. 4 (1964), also in *Image, Music, Text*, trans. Stephen Heath (Fontana/Collins, Glasgow, 1977). Seminal influence on so-called 'deep' qualitative content analysis of pictures.

Bartlett, C.F. *Remembering: A Study in Experimental and Social Psychology* (Cambridge University Press, London, 1932). A classic study of important psychological processes.

Gombrich, E.H. *Art and Illusion: A Study in the Psychology of Pictorial Representation* (Phaidon Press, Oxford, 1960).

Gombrich, E.H. *The Sense of Order: A Study in the Psychology of Decorative Art* (Phaidon Press, Oxford, 1979). These two books are companions; the first dealing with the psychology of pictorial representation and the second dealing with pattern perception. They are essential reading for anyone interested in pursuing this field further. Gombrich is erudite and profound in his insights but can be infuriatingly vague while remaining compellingly readable.

Hartley, James. *Designing Instructional Text* (Kogan Page, London, 1978). Useful as a guide to the economies which can be made in printing instructional texts by attention to careful design. Not very useful in giving pedagogic advice.

Ivins, William J. Jr. *Prints and Visual Communication* (Harvard University Press, Cambridge, Mass., 1953). It is a great shame that the ideas in the early chapters of this book are not developed fully through a wide selection of historical material. The history of visual communication remains to be written but this book does provide some useful pointers.

Kepes, Gyorgy. *Language of Vision* (Paul Theobold, Chicago 1969, first published 1944). A classic text which clearly demonstrates the exaggerated stance which emerged from the Bauhaus basic design course.

Macdonald-Ross, Michael. 'How Numbers are Shown: A Review of Research on the Presentation of Quantitative Data in Texts',

190 Annotated Bibliography

Audio-Visual Communication Review, vol. 25 (1977), pp. 359-409. Important source of information for designers with some useful warnings to over-eager researchers.

Macdonald-Ross, Michael and Smith, Eleanor. 'Graphics in Text: a Bibliography', *IET Monograph No. 6* (Institute of Educational Technology, The Open University, Milton Keynes, 1977). A useful bibliography on sources of ideas and research on graphics in text. The only good guide to the literature available.

Neisser, U. *Cognitive Psychology* (Appelton-Century-Crofts, New York, 1967). Clear and lucid development of many of the concepts which are used in this book.

Salomon, Gavriel. *Interaction of Media, Cognition and Learning* (Jossey-Bass, San Francisco, 1979). Despite the heavy empirical basis of this book — essentially a series of quasi-laboratory experiments — the ideas are well worth serious consideration.

Schramm, Wilber. *Big Media, Little Media: Tools and Technologies for Instruction.* (Sage Publications, Inc., Beverly Hills, California, 1977). A not very comforting assessment of educational technology but one which should be essential reading to all involved in educational technology.

Stewart, Ann Harleman. *Graphic Representation of Models in Linguistic Theory* (Indiana University Press, Bloomington, 1976). Studies of this kind are rare and despite a number of weaknesses it is an area of research which needs encouraging. This study provides some insight into the relation between basic scientific research and visual communication.

Wright, Patricia. 'The Quality Control of Document Design', *Information Design Journal,* vol. 1, no. 1 (1979), pp. 33-42. The most straightforward account of research strategies available in document design. Unfortunately the concept of 'quality control' is a little inappropriate.

Yates, Frances A. *The Art of Memory* (Penguin Books, Harmondsworth, Middlesex, 1978). The power of the visual to sustain complex intellectual activity in an area of forgotten scholarship is revealed in this fascinating book which traces the history of memory systems from ancient Greece to the seventeenth century.

Useful Journals

Information Design Journal. Robert Waller. Institute of Educational Technology, The Open University, Walton Hall, Milton Keynes MK7 6AA.

Studies in Visual Communication. PO Box 13358, Philadelphia, PA 19010, USA.

REFERENCES

Albarn, Keith and Smith, Jenny Miall. *Diagram: The Instrument of Thought* (Thames and Hudson, London, 1977).

Albers, Josef. *Interaction of Color* (Yale University Press, New Haven, 1975).

Anschutz, Richard. 'August Kekule' in Farber, E. (ed.) *Great Chemists* (Interscience Publishers, New York, 1961), p. 700.

Aristotle, *The 'Art' of Rhetoric*, trans. by John Henry Freese (William Heinemann, London, 1926).

Arnheim, Rudolph. *Art and Visual Perception* (Faber and Faber, London, 1956).

—— 'Expressions', *Art Education* (March 1978), pp. 37, 38.

Asimov, Isaac. *Asimov's Biographical Encyclopedia of Science and Technology* (Pan Books, London, 1975).

Ayer, A.J. *The Problem of Knowledge* (Penguin Books, Harmondsworth, Middlesex, 1956).

Balchin, W.G.V. and Coleman, Alice M. 'Graphicacy should be the Fourth Ace in the Pack', *Times Educational Supplement*, 5 Nov. 1965.

Banham, Reyner.*Theory and Design in the First Machine Age* (The Architectural Press, London, 1960).

Barthes, Roland. *Elements of Semiology*, trans. Annette Levers and Colin Smith (Hill and Wang, New York, 1967a).

—— 'Rhetorique de l'Image', *Communications*, vol. 4 (1964), also in *Image, Music, Text*, trans. Stephen Heath (Fontana/Collins, Glasgow, 1977).

—— *Systeme de la mode* (Seuil, Paris, 1967b).

Bartlett, C.F. *Remembering: A Study in Experimental and Social Psychology* (Cambridge University Press, London, 1932).

Baynes, Ken and Pugh, Francis. 'Introduction' in *The Art of the Engineer*, catalogue of Welsh Arts Council Touring Exhibition (Welsh Arts Council, Cardiff, 1978).

Berelson, Bernard. *Content Analysis in Communication Research* (Glencoe Free Press, New York, 1952).

Blumler, Jay G. 'Producers' Attitude towards Television Coverage of an Election Campaign: a Case Study' in Halmos, Paul (ed.) 'The Sociology of Mass Media Communicators', *The Sociological*

Review Monograph 13 (University of Keele, 1969).

Bonsiepe, Guy. 'Persuasive Communication: Towards a Visual Rhetoric', *Uppercase* 5 (Whitefriars, London 1961), pp. 19-34.

—— 'Visual/Verbal Rhetoric', *Ulm* (1965), pp. 14-16.

Bower, T.G.R. 'Discrimination of Depth in Premotor Infants', *Psychonomic Science*, vol. 1 (1964), p. 368.

—— 'The Object in the World of the Infant', *Scientific American*, vol. 225, (1971), pp. 30-8.

Brinton, W.C. 'Graphic Methods of Presenting Facts', *Engineering Magazine* (New York, 1916).

Bruner, J.S. and Olson, D.R. 'Learning through Experience and Learning through Media' in Gerbner, G., Gross, L.P. and Melody, W.H. (eds.) *Communication Technology and Social Policy* (John Wiley, New York, 1973), pp. 209-27.

Burns, Tom. 'Public Service and Private World', *The Sociological Review Monograph*, 13 (University of Keele, 1969).

Cairney, Peter and Sless, David. 'Understanding Symbolic Signs: Design Guidelines Based on User Responses', *Proceedings of the 17th Annual Conference of the Ergonomics Society of Australia and New Zealand* (Sydney, 1980).

Chomsky, Noam. Review of B.F. Skinner's *'Verbal Behaviour'*, *Language*, vol. 35 (1959), pp. 26-58.

—— *Aspects of the Theory of Syntax* (MIT Press, Cambridge, Mass., 1965).

Coward, Rosalind and Ellis, John. *Language and Materialism* (Routledge and Kegan Paul, London, 1977).

Dale, E. *Audiovisual Methods in Teaching*, 3rd edn (Holt, Rinehart and Winston, New York, 1969).

De Leeuw, Manya and De Leeuw, Eric. *Read Better, Read Faster* (Penguin Books, Harmondsworth, 1965).

Dondis, Denis A. *A Primer in Visual Literacy* (MIT Press, Cambridge, Mass., 1973).

Duchastel, Philippe, C. 'Illustrating Instructional Texts', *Educational Technology*, vol. 18, no. 11 (1978), pp. 36-9.

Duchastel, Philippe and Waller, Robert. 'Pictorial Illustration in Instructional Texts', *Educational Technology*, vol. 19, no. 11 (1979), pp. 20-5.

Duncum, Paul. 'Children's Spontaneous Image-making as Play', *The Official Journal of the Institute of Art Education*, vol. 3, no. 1 (May 1980), pp. 1-33.

Eco, Umberto. ' Componental Analysis of the Architectural Sign/

Column', *Semiotica*, vol. V, no. 2 (1972).

—— *A Theory of Semiotics* (Macmillan, London, 1977).

Eells, W.C. 'The Relative Merits of Circles and Bars for Representing Component Parts', *Journal of the American Statistical Association* vol. 21 (1926), pp. 119-32.

Elliott, Philip. *The Making of a Television Series: a Case Study in the Sociology of Culture* (Constable, London, 1972).

Evans-Pritchard, E.E. 'For Example Witchcraft' from E.E. Evans-Pritchard, *Witchcraft, Oracles and Magic among the Azande* (Clarendon Press, London, 1937). Abridged for Mary Douglas (ed.) *Rules and Meaning* (Penguin Education, Harmondsworth, Middlesex, 1973).

Fiske, John and Hartley, John. *Reading Television* (Methuen & Co., London, 1978).

Fleming, M.L. 'Classification and Analysis of Instructional Illustrations', *A V Communication Review*, vol. 15 (1967), pp. 246-56.

—— 'On Pictures in Educational Research', *Instructional Science*, vol. 8 (1979), pp. 235-51.

Foucault, Michel. *Language, Counter-Memory, Practice* (Cornell University Press and Basil Blackwell, Oxford, 1977).

Gagné, Robert M. and Briggs, Leslie. *Principles of Instructional Design* (Holt, Rinehart and Winston, Inc., New York, 1974).

Gans, Herber J. *Deciding What's News: a Study of CBS Evening News, NBC Nightly News, Newsweek, and Time* (Pantheon Books, New York, 1979).

Garland, Ken. 'Some General Characteristics Present in Diagrams Denoting Activity, Event and Relationship', *Information Design Journal*, vol. 1, no. 1 (1979).

Gerbner, G. 'Violence and Television Drama: Trends and Symbolic Functions' in Costock, George and Rubenstein, E. (eds.) *Media Content and Control.* The Surgeon General's Report (US Government Printing Office, Washington D.C., 1972) pp. 28-187.

Gibson, J.J. *The Senses Considered as Perceptual Systems* (Houghton, Mifflin, Boston, 1966).

—— 'The Information Available in Pictures', *Leonardo*, vol. 4 (1971), pp. 27-35.

Goffman, Erving. *Gender Advertisements* (Macmillan, London, 1979).

Golding, Peter. *The Mass Media* (Longmans, London, 1974).

Golding, Peter and Elliott, Philip. *Making the News* (Centre for Mass Communication Research, University of Leicester, 1976).

Gombrich, E.H. *Art and Illusion: A Study in the Psychology of Pictorial Representation* (Phaidon Press, London, 1960).
—— *The Sense of Order: A Study in the Psychology of Decorative Art* (Phaidon Press, Oxford, 1979).
Gordon, William J. *Synectics: the Development of Creative Capacity* (Harper and Row, New York, 1961).
Guiraud, P. *Semiology* (Routledge and Kegan Paul, London, 1975).
Haber, Ralph Norman and Hershenson, Maurice. *The Psychology of Visual Perception* (Holt, Rinehart and Winston, London, 1974).
Hadamard, J. *An Essay on The Psychology of Invention in the Mathematical Field* (Princeton University Press, Princeton, N.J., 1945).
Hartley, James. *Designing Instructional Text* (Kogan Page, London, 1978).
Hawkes, Terence. *Structuralism and Semiotics* (Methuen & Co. Ltd, London, 1977).
Hewish, Antony. 'Pulsars', *Scientific American*, vol. 219, no. 4 (1968), pp. 25-35.
Hochberg, J. and Brooks, V. 'Pictorial Recognition as an Unlearnt Ability: A Study of One Child's Performance', *American Journal of Psychology*, vol. 75 (1962), pp. 624-8.
Hovland, Carl Iver, Lumsdaid, Arthur and Sheffield, Fredd. *Experiments in Mass Communication* (Princeton University Press, Princeton, N.J., 1949).
Itten, Johannes. *Design and Form; the Basic Course at the Bauhaus* (Revised and updated by Anneliese Itten; tr. from German by Fred Bradley) (Thames and Hudson, London, 1975).
Ivins, William M. Jr. *Prints and Visual Communication* (Harvard University Press, Cambridge, Mass., 1953).
Jones, Christopher J. *Design Methods: Seeds of Human Futures* (John Wiley, London, 1970).
Jones, Greta, Connel, Ian and Meadows, Jack. *The Presentation of Science by the Media* (Primary Communications Research Centre, University of Leicester, 1978).
Kant, Immanuel. *Critique of Pure Reason*, trans. Norman Kemp Smith (Macmillan & Co. Ltd, New York, 1964).
Karsten, K.G. *Charts and Graphs: An Introduction to Graphic Methods in the Control and Analysis of Statistics* (Prentice-Hall, Englewood Cliffs, N.J., 1923).
Katz, J. and Fodor, J.A. 'The Structure of a Semantic Theory', *Language*, vol. 39 (1963), pp. 170-210.

Kennedy, John M. *A Psychology of Picture Perception* (Jossey-Bass, San Francisco, 1974).

Kepes, Gyorgy. *Language of Vision* (Paul Theobold, Chicago, 1969, first published 1944).

Key, Wilson, Bryan. *Subliminal Seduction: Ad. Media's Manipulation of a Not so Innocent America* (Prentice Hall, Englewood Cliffs, N.J., 1973).

Kinross, Robin. Review article: '*Designing Instructional Text* by James Hartley', *Instructional Science*, vol. 8 (1979), pp. 275-89.

Klapper, Joseph T. *The Effects of Mass Communication* (Princeton University Press, Princeton, N.J., 1949).

Klee, Paul. *Pedagogical Sketchbook*, intro. and trans. Sibyl Moholy-Nagy (Faber, London, 1972).

Knowlton, J.Q. 'On the Definition of a "Picture"', *A V Communication Review*, vol. 14 (1966), pp. 157-83.

Koffka, K. *The Principles of Gestalt Psychology* (Harcourt, Brace and World, New York, 1935).

Leach, Edmund. *Culture and Communication: the Logic by which Symbols are Connected* (Cambridge University Press, London, 1976).

Lesser, Gerald S. *Children and Television: Lessons from Sesame Street* (Random House, New York, 1974).

Lévi-Strauss, Claude. *(Mythologiques): Introduction to a Science of Mythology*. tr. from French by John and Doreen Weightman (Cape, London, 1979, 3 vols.).

Leymore, Varda, Langholz. *Hidden Myth: Structure and Symbolism in Advertising* (Basic Books Inc., New York, 1975).

Lowenfeld, Viktor and Brittain, W.L. *Creativity and Mental Growth* (Macmillan, New York, 1970 (1st edn 1947)).

McQuail, Denis. 'Uncertainty about the Audience, and the Organization of Mass Communications', *The Sociological Review Monograph 13* (1969).

MacCorquodale, Kenneth. 'On Chomsky's review of Skinner's *Verbal Behaviour*', *Journal of the Experimental Analysis of Behaviour*, vol. 13, no. 1 (1970), pp. 83-99.

Macdonald-Ross, Michael. 'How Numbers are Shown: a Review of Research on the Presentation of Quantitative Data in Texts', *Audio-Visual Communication Review*, vol. 25 (1977), pp. 359-409.

—— 'Scientific Diagrams and the Generation of Plausible Hypotheses: An Essay in the History of ideas', *Instructional Science*, vol. 8 (1979), pp. 223-34.

Macdonald-Ross, Michael and Waller, Robert, 'The Transformer', *Penrose Annual*, vol. 69 (1976), pp. 141-52.

Macdonald-Ross, Michael and Smith, Eleanor. 'Graphics in Text: a Bibliography', *IET monograph No. 6* (Institute of Educational Technology, The Open University, Milton Keynes, 1977).

Meihoefer, Hans-Joachim. 'The Utility of the Circle as an Effective Cartographic Symbol', *The Canadian Cartographer*, vol. 6, no. 2 (1969), pp. 105-17.

—— 'The Visual Perception of the Circle in Thematic Maps: Experimental Results', *Canadian Cartographer*, vol. 10, no. 1 (1973).

Metz, Christian. *Film Language: a Semiotics of the Cinema*, trans. Michael Taylor (Oxford University Press, New York, 1974).

Millum, Trevor. *Images of Woman; Advertising in Women's Magazines* (Chatto & Windus, London, 1975).

Moholy-Nagy, Laszlo. *The New Vision; Fundamentals of Design, Printing, Sculpture, Architecture*, trans. Dephne M. Hoffman (Norton, New York, 1938).

Morison, Stanley. *First Principles of Typography*, 2nd edn (Cambridge Authors' and Printers' Guides 1, University Press, Cambridge, 1967).

Neisser, U. *Cognitive Psychology* (Appelton-Century-Crofts, New York, 1967).

—— *Cognition and Reality* (W.H. Freeman and Company, San Francisco, 1976).

Neurath, O. *International Picture Language* (Kegan Paul, London, 1936).

Oakley, Graham. *The Church Mouse* (Macmillan, London, 1972).

O'Connor, N. and Hermelin, B. 'Life and Cross-Modality Recognition in Subnormal Children', *Quarterly Journal of Experimental Psychology*, vol. 11 (1961), pp. 48-52.

Paivio, A. 'Imagery and Long-term Memory', *in Kennedy A. and Wilkes A. (eds.) Studies in Long-term Memory* (John Wiley, New York, 1975).

Peirce, Charles Sanders. *Collected Papers of Charles Sanders Peirce*, 8 vols. Edited by Charles Hartshorne, Paul Weiss and Arthur Burks (Harvard University Press, Cambridge, Mass., 1931-58).

Polyak, Stephen Lucian. *The Vertebrate Visual System*, ed. Heinrich Kluiver (Chicago University Press, Chicago, 1968).

Pritchard, Roy. 'Stabilized Images on the Retina', *Scientific American*, vol. 204, no. 6 June (1961), pp. 72-8.

Read, H. *Education Through Art* (Faber & Faber, London, 1958 (1st edn 1943)).

Roberts, Don D. *The Existential Graphs of Charles S. Peirce* (Mouton, The Hague, 1973).

Salomon, Gavriel. *Interaction of Media, Cognition and Learning* (Jossey-Bass, San Francisco, 1979).

de Sausmarez, Maurice. *Basic Design: the Dynamics of Visual Form* (Studio Vista, London, 1964).

de Saussure, Ferdinand. *Course in General Linguistics*, trans. Wade Baskin (Fontana/Collins, Glasgow, 1974).

Schlesinger, Philip. *Putting 'Reality' Together* (Constable, London, 1978).

Schramm, Wilber. *Big Media, Little Media: Tools and Technologies for Instruction* (Sage Publications, Inc., Beverly Hills, California, 1977).

Sebeok, Thomas A. *Contributions to the Doctrine of Signs* (Peter de Ridder Press, Lisse, 1976).

Sless, David. 'Editorial. *Big Media, Little Media*', *Pivot: A Journal of South Australian Education*, vol. 5, no. 4 (1978), pp. 3-6.

Sless, David. *Visual Thinking* (Radio University 5UV, University of Adelaide, South Australia 1978 (reprinted 1980)).

—— 'Image Design and Modification: an Experimental Project in Transforming', *Information Design Journal*, vol. 1, no. 2 (1979), pp. 74-80.

Smith, W. Eugene. 'Photographic Journalism', *Photo Notes* (June 1948), pp. 4-5 in *Photographers on Photography*, ed. Nathan Lyons (Prentice-Hall, Englewood Cliffs, N.J., 1966), pp. 103-5.

Snyder, Benson, R. *The Hidden Curriculum* (MIT Press, Cambridge, Mass., 1973).

Spencer, H. *The Visible Word* (Lund Humphries, London, 1969).

Stewart, Ann Harleman. *Graphic Representation of Models in Linguistic Theory* (Indiana University Press, Bloomington, 1976).

Steiglitz, Alfred. 'The Hand Camera — Its Present Importance', *The American Annual of Photography* (1897), pp. 18-27. In *Photographers on Photography*, ed. Nathan Lyons (Prentice-Hall), Englewood Cliffs, N.J., 1966), pp. 108-10.

Storer, R.G. and Cahill, R.T. *Personal Communication*, 1978.

Sturrock, John (ed.) *Structuralism and Since: From Levi-Strauss to Derrida* (Oxford University Press, Oxford, 1979).

Susman, Gerald I. and Evered, Roger D. 'An Assessment of the Scientific Merits of Action Research', *Administrative Science Quarterly*, vol. 23, no. 4 (1978), pp. 582-602.

Szarkowski, J. *Looking at Photographs: 100 pictures from the Collection of the Museum of Modern Art* (Museum of Modern Art, New York, 1973).

Tinker, Miles A. *Legibility of Print* (University of Minnesota Press, Minnesota, 1965).

Twyman, Michael. 'A Schema for the Study of Graphic Languages' in Bouma, H., Kolers, P. and Wrolstad, M. (eds.) *Processing of Visible Language 1*. (Plenum, New York, 1979).

—— 'The Significance of ISOTYPE', *Graphic Communication Through ISOTYPE* (University of Reading, 1975).

Watson, James Dewey. *The Double Helix; a Personal Account of the Discovery of the Structure of DNA* (Weidenfeld and Nicolson, London, 1968).

Welsh Arts Council. *The Art of the Engineer* (Welsh Arts Council Touring Exhibition Catalogue, 1978).

Weston, Edward. 'Seeing Photographically', *The Complete Photographer*, vol. 9, no. 49, 1943, pp. 3200-6 in *Photographers on Photography*, ed. Nathan Lyons (Prentice-Hall, Inc. Englewood Cliffs, N.J., 1966), pp. 159-63.

Williamson, Judith. *Decoding Advertisements: Ideology and Meaning in Advertising* (Marian Boyars, London, 1978).

Wilson, Brent and Wilson, Marjorie. 'An Iconoclastic View of the Imagery Sources in the Drawings of Young People', *Art Education* (January 1977), pp. 5-11.

Wright, Patricia. 'The Quality Control of Document Design', *Information Design Journal*, vol. 1, no. 1 (1979), pp. 33-42.

Yates, Frances A. *The Art of Memory* (Penguin Books, Harmondsworth, Middlesex, 1978).

INDEX

abstraction 118-22 *passim*
action research 177, 199
advertisements 43, 125; decoding 65;
for cheap cameras 75; meaning 108;
photographs used in 103-4
advertising 39, 42-6 *passim*, 124-5,
128; agency 42, 45; annual turnover
46; audience research 44-5; clients
46; contemporary critique of 124-5;
effective 46; maintaining credibility
46; research departments 39; rhetorical role 101
Albarn, Keith 162, 192
Albers, Joseph 51, 192
algebra 147
algorithms 143, 148
aliens 38
analysis 165, 175
animation of the inanimate 113
Anschutz, Richard 131, 192
anthropology 167
architecture 64, 89-90
Arecibo message 35-45 *passim*, 72,
141
Aristotle 25, 192
Arnheim, Rudolph 53, 78, 192
art 39, 74-7; communicating arts 40;
education 55, 63, 76, 183; educators
50, 55, 78; galleries 77, 100; historians 23, 122; non-figurative 71;
realism 94; room 76; teaching in art
can damage the mind 76
artificial energy 37; *see also* Pulsars
artists 76; applying a schema 121,
academy education 51; *see also*
painter
Asimov, Isaac 147, 192
astronomers 25, 30
attention 33-4
attentional illustrations 106, 107-11;
advertising 108-9; definition 106;
relation 107; role 109
audience 27-8, 35, 37-49 *passim*, 54,
113-14, 165, 169, 182-4; anonymous 44; comprehension 39; ignorance 46; inferences about 144; inferred audience 35, 37-41, 44-5, 62,
87, 113-14, 184; isolation from 177;

knowledge of 38-44 *passim*, 167;
logical imperative to construct 44;
passivity 113, 165; reaction 113;
research 40, 44-5, 48-9, 177
audience/message relation 25-30 *passim*, 33-4, 38-44 *passim*, 47-8, 54,
62-3, 77, 79, 87-8, 94, 97, 100-4
passim, 107, 123-4, 130, 138, 148,
165-9 *passim*, 179, 181, 182-4; and
cognitive skills 130; and content
analysis 43; and surrogate audience
47; as unit of analysis 25-30, 33, 79;
conflation with author/message relation 44, 88; definition 181; education 77; effectiveness 44; engineering drawing 138; explanation and
description 123-4; inferred author
in 41; in Gestalt psychology 54; in
photography 94, 100, 104; in preindustrial society 48; in typography
165-9; new model of communication
25; reading 169; rules governing 34;
separation from author/message relation 62, 94; similarity to author/
message relation 38; taxonomy of
107; *see also* author/message relation
audio-visual: aids 76; department 47;
specialists 89; unit 42
author 25-8 *passim*, 72, 123-4, 169,
182-4; authorship 26-7; errors of
judgement of 62; inferred author 26-
8, 41, 67, 75, 87, 94, 105, 113-14,
165, 184; integrity 124; intentions
113
author/message relation 25-40 *passim*,
42-62 *passim*, 71-2, 79, 88, 97-100
passim, 114, 123, 128, 138, 165,
181-4; and pictures 71-2; as unit of
analysis 25-33, 79; conflation with
audience/message relation 44, 88;
definition 181; description and explanation 123; engineering drawing
138; inferred audience in 35-8, 40;
in photography 97-100; in typography 165; new model of communication 25; Open University texts
114; professional practice 48-9;
understanding of 42; *see also* Basic

200